1930s

NEW YORK TIMES (365)

STEPHEN BOEK

ISBN 978-1-63784-076-4 (paperback)
ISBN 978-1-63784-077-1 (digital)

Hawes & Jenkins Publishing
16427 N Scottsdale Road Suite 410
Scottsdale, AZ 85254
www.hawesjenkins.com

Printed in the United States of America

1930: NEW YORK TIMES (365)

JANUARY

Republicans Pledge Aid To Governor On Prisons On Eve Of 1930 Session

Governor Stiffens Water Power Plan In Message Read To The Legislature; Wants Crime Breeding In Prisons Ended

Byrd Geologist Discovers Coal Strip On Mt. Nansen Inlaid In Sandstone Cap

Fire Menaces The Capitol But Is Quickly Subdued; Historic Documents Saved

Senate Factions Agree To Put Tariff To Front; Bar Prohibition Debate

Republican Rift Widens As Macy Demands Maier Quit State Leadership

Hoover Speeds Delegates To Navy Conference Today; Hopes For Real Reduction

Hoover Says Advance Of World Peace Rests On Navy Conference At London; Tells Hopes At Farewell To Delegates

Our Delegates Sail Today For London Naval Parley, Confident Of An Accord

Washington Ready For Wide Navy Cuts In Agreement With MacDonald's Plans; Our Delegates Sail With High Hopes

Law Enforcement Fails, Wickersham Board Finds; Full Report On Monday

Snowden Warns Germans To Stop Needless Delays And Accept Young Plan

Britain Sees Peace Pacts Real Basis For Navy Cuts; Sends Reply To France

Hoover Urges Congress To Rebuild Dry Law Enforcement Machinery; Backs Message With Board's Reports

Republican Power Bill Approved By Roosevelt; 10-Year Deadlock Ended

Abolition Of Battleships By All Powers Of World Is Urged By MacDonald

Blaine Moves For Repeal As Wets And Drys Battle In Both Senate And House

Stimson Hastens To See MacDonald; Battleship Issue To Fore In London; Washington Doubts Ban Will Be Placed

Washington Might Scrap Battleships To The Extent Of Cuts By Britain, But Abolition Is Not On Our Program

Stimson Cheered By Parley Prospects After Meeting French And Italians; Issue Of Battleships Is Made Clear

Stimson Pledges Success Of Parley At Dinner Of Welcome By Britain; King Opens The Conference Today

Work Starts For Navy Limitation After World Hears King Open Parley; Stimson Presses Effort For Unity

Powers Bar Disputes At Parley Today; Will Spend Week In Cautious Approach; Cruisers Likely To Be First On List

Stimson Presents No Details Offer As Conference Opens; Stands On Parity With Britain; Other Aims Are Stated

Security Pledges Urged To Obtain Cuts In Navies; Our Aid Will Be Sought

$1,000,000,000 Saving Likely In New Battleship Holiday, Now Chief Issue At London

Eielson Plane Found A Wreck In Siberia; Bodies Of 2 Fliers Believed Under Snow; Food They Carried Untouched In Cabin

Mitchell Bans Drinkers In Dry Enforcement Jobs; Senators Attack Chiefs

Spanish Dictator Quits; Parliament To Be Elected; King Acts To Guard Throne

First Wet Bill Hearings Since Prohibition Came In Set By House Committee

Committee To Draft Plan Of Compromise At London; Italy Defers Parity Bid

FEBRUARY

Phone Rates Cut 20 Per Cent By Utility Board's Order, Making A $3,000,000 Slash

Tardieu Tests The Pace In London Conference; Outlook Now Promising

Stimson Prepares To Tell Our Minimum Naval Needs; Transfer Concession Seen

President Names Hughes Chief Justice As Taft Resigns Because Of Ill Health When Trip To Asheville Fails To Aid Him

Stimson And British Agree To Scrap 8 Battleships Now And Build None Until 1936

Assassin Wounds President Ortiz Rubio Soon After 50,000 See Him Take The Oath; Wide Plot For Coup Charged To Rivals

Stimson Gives Out Naval Program, Parity With Britain At 15 Battleships And Right Of Duplication In Cruisers

British Would Abolish Battleships; Submit Plans For Naval Cuts Now And Further Reduction At 1935 Parley

House Approves Dry Shift To Department Of Justice, First Of Hoover Reforms

France Disturbed By Move To Condemn Submarines At
Conference Tomorrow

186 Indicted In Rum Plot By Grand Jury In Chicago; Hotel
Manager Here Raided

Blasts And Fire Wreck Liner Muenchen; Ship Sinks At Pier,
Imperils Hudson Tube; 2 Killed In Explosions; Loss $2,000,000

Senate Battles All Day Over Hughes Nomination; Confirmation
Today Seen

Hughes Confirmed By Senate, 52 To 26; Vote Comes At End Of
Four Day Fight; He Restates Ideals Of Public Service

Increase By Britain Looms To Meet French Program; Hope For
Navy Cuts Wanes

Bar Asks Vitale Removal On Corruption Charges; Court Hearing
Set For Him

Byrd Ship, Blown Far West, Gains Shelter Of Barrier And Heads
For Her Goal

Tardieu Cabinet Falls On Minor Issue, Holding Up French Part In
Navy Parley; We May Move To Bolster Kellogg Pact

7 Killed, 61 Hurt In Blasts In Jersey Alcohol Plant; Many Victims
May Be Blind

Byrd Party On Ship Homeward Bound; City Of New York Loaded
Over Night; Polar Plane Left At Antarctic Base

Coudert Sees 'Civil War' If 'Real' Attempt Is Made To Enforce The
Dry Law

Grundy Calls On Old Guard To Halt Coalition Tariff; Sees Hoover Aiding Cuts

Hoover Compromise Move Expected In Tariff Fight; Watson Cheerful On Bill

Briand Ready To Accept Hoover Security Pledge Without Senate Approval

Hoover Warns Congress To Economize Or Be Faced By Tax Rise Of 40 Per Cent

Senators Assail Hoover On Warning To Economize As He Denies Criticism

Dry Law Repeal Urged By Atterbury And Others Before House Committee

Cry 'Down With The King', Wave Red Flag In Madrid; Rioters And Police Clash

MARCH

5-Cent Fare Held Binding Even If It Is Unprofitable; I.R.T. Loses In State Court

'Home Rule' For States Demanded By Roosevelt; Reaffirms Liquor Stand

Woll Lays Red Riots Here To World Plot Of Soviet; Stalin For Curb In Russia

Senators Demand Action To Check Unemployment; Hoover's Stand Attacked

Fess Lauds Hoover's Year, Answering Senate Critics On Tariff And Prohibition

Drys Portray Prohibition As Basis Of Prosperity; Edison And Ford For Law

Reds Battle Police In Union Square; Scores Injured, Leaders Are Seized; Two Dead, Many Hurt In Clashes Abroad

More Work, Says Hoover, And Depression Is Passing; 36 States Are Now Normal

Ex-President Taft Dies At Capital, Succumbing To Many Weeks' Illness, Five Hours After Justice Sanford

Byrd And His Men Reach New Zealand; Welcoming Cheers Mark
The Return Of The Expedition From The Antarctic

Whalen Tells Employers Of 300 Reds They Hired; All Will Be
Discharged

Taft Borne To Arlington, Receives Soldier's Burial As The Nation
Pays Homage

Prohibition Stands Test Say Scores Of Women Drys, 'Speaking For
12,000,000'

Ninth Planet Discovered On Edge Of Solar System; First Found In
84 Years

Basis For 3-Power Treaty In Agreement With Japan Announced By
Americans

Move For 5-Power Treaty Goes On With Tardieu's Aid; He Bids For
British Help

Churches Here Denounce Soviet War On Religion; Thousands Join
In Prayer

Dry Enforcement Gaining And Corruption Declines, Wickersham
Testifies

Governor Cuts $12,000,000 From Budget; Veto Assails Items
Republicans Put In

Taft Shifted To Dry Side, Brother Says At Hearing; Others Praise
Prohibition

Roper Urges A Dry Council, With 7-Year Truce By Wets, To Give
Law A Fair Trial

Won't Resign, Says Whalen After A Talk With Mayor; Rumor Had Him Out May 2

Senate Completes Revision Of Tariff After Weary Fight Of 6 Months, 18 Days; Final Vote Is Deferred Till Tomorrow

Hoover Board Tells Facts Of The Business Situation; Retarding Factors Fading

Senate Passes Tariff Bill, 53 To 31, After Opponents Assail Rate Boosts; House To Act On Conference In Week

Stimson Again Bars Any Security Pact; Would Consider Consultative Pledge With No Obligation Of Military Aid

Liquor 'Control' Failure, Says Ontario Ex-Premier; Cites Rise In Lawlessness

New Move For All-European Peace Pact Under Way In View Of American Stand; Senators See Bar To Conference Pledge

We Will Set Strict Limits To Any Consultation Pact; French For Pacific Model

Hoover Is In Full Accord With Delegates In London; Tokio To Accept New Ratio

French Ask British Pledge To Act On League's Advice; Italy Joins In Opposition

APRIL

Stimson Urges Agreement Of Briand And M'Donald, But 3-Power Idea Grows

Yancey Plane Is Down Off Bermuda; Sea Calm, Don't Worry, Crew's Word; Plan To Finish The Trip This Morning

Yancey Reaches Bermuda; Tells Of Night In Plane And Take-Off From Ocean

No 5-Power Pact, Says Italy If France Refuses Parity; Mussolini Will Not Yield

Americans Put Pressure On Parley As Hope Wanes; New Hitch With Japanese

Briand Takes New Plans On Security To Tardieu; Hope For Treaty Revives

Board Plans To Sacrifice Five-Cent Fare Clause To Save The Transit Bill

France Against 5-Power Treaty Now, Preferring To Stay Out If Italy Does; M'Donald Meets Threat In Commons

Mrs. M'Cormick Is Winner Over Deneen In Primary For Illinois Senatorship

France And Italy Are Out Of Main Treaty But may Sign Two Other Accords

Three-Power Agreement Is Reached And London Parley Will Adjourn With Way Open For Others To Join

Hoover Hails Naval Parley's Success; Points To Big Savings For US And Others And Sees End Of Competitive Building

Naval Experts Draft Plan For Scrapping Battleships; Britain Seeks Safeguards

Stimson Predicts Further Naval Cuts Will Follow London's Achievements; Hails Limitation And End To Rivalry

Hoover Sure We Will Enter World Court, He Tells D.A.R., Which Has Opposed It; Stresses Our Duty To Maintain Peace

Fierce Riots In Calcutta With Mobs Barricaded; Ten Europeans Injured

Curran Defends Wets Under Heavy Fire; Revolt Is Justified, He Tells Senators; Beer Permit Bribe Hint In Trial Here

Hoover Sounds Senators On Navy Treaty; Borah Indicates He Is For Ratification; Pact Is Completed For Signing Tuesday

Hoover Pictured In Doubt Of Enforcing The Dry Law; Obey It, Says Wickersham

Gunmen Invade Prison, Arm Convicts; 2 Die, 3 Hurt As Outbreak Is Quelled

Lindbergh Sets A Record From Coast Of 14 3/4 Hours With Wife As Navigator; Flies 180 Miles An Hour At 14,000 Feet

335 Convicts Die In Ohio Prison Fire; Troops Subdue 2,000 Free In The Yard; Three Other Fires Set In Escape Plot

Delay In Freeing Convicts Trapped By Fire Revealed By Inquiry; 317 Perished

30 Killed In Indian Fights, Spread Over Wide Areas; Mob Burns Soldiers In Car

Ontario's Dry Law Failed, Says Liquor Control Head; Roper Says Students Drink

Seize 11 Hip Flask Patrons In Broadway Night Club; New Federal Raid Policy

Whalen Won't Aid Hip-Flask Campaign; Doran Approves It

Better Trade Conditions In All Lines Portrayed By Hoover Survey Head

Hoover Demands Passage Of Dry Enforcement Bills; Stresses Need In Message

Hoover Backs Mass Drive To Stamp Out Crime Rings Linked To Liquor Traffic

MAY

Hoover Gets Naval Treaty; Senate Favor Is Indicated By Reception Of Robinson

Worst Of Depression Over, Says Hoover, With Cooperation Lessening Distress; Plans Study To Avert Future Crises

Hoover 'Not Dry At Heart,' Stayton Said In Letter; Denies Giving Wet Party

Farm Debenture Rejected In House Under Veto Hit; Flexible Tariff Retained

Gandhi Seized By British For Indefinite Detention; Troops Posted For Crisis

Fires Gain In South Jersey; Other Areas Winning Fight; Hunt For Incendiaries On

Bishop Cannon Got $65,300 To Use In Defeating Smith; Asked Name Be Concealed

Senate Rejects Judge Parker, 41 To 39; Spirited Attack By Johnson Precedes Final Vote On Hoover's Choice For Bench

Gandhi Forces Seize City In Fierce Fight; 25 Killed; British Rush More Troops

Troops Fire On Texas Mob, Wounding Two In Battle After Burning Of Negro

Civil War Raging In China On 170-Mile Battle Front; Nanking In Grave Peril

Treaty Contest On Today; Naval Experts Divided On Key Issue Of Cruisers

Stimson Challenges Foes Of Naval Pact On Parity, Opening Senate Hearings

Home Brewing Is Lawful, Sometimes, Says M'Bride; League Aids Drinking Drys

Senate Treaty Critics Press Attack, Sharply Examining Stimson And Adams; Pratt Explains Shift To 6-Inch Guns

Morrow Demands Repeal Of Dry Law With Control Of Liquor Left To States; Opens Race For Senate In Newark

Whalen Successor Chosen, Walker Says On His Return; Shift Expected On Tuesday

Full Text Of Briand's Pan-European Plan; Federal Union Under League Proposed For All Matters Of Common Interest

Zeppelin Nearing Spain On Way To South America; Flying Fast, 1,000 Feet Up

Senate Drops Debenture And Its Flexible Tariff; Ends Impasse With House

Mulrooney Heads Police; 34 Years On The Force; Whalen Farewell Today

Hoover Applies Pressure For Passage Of Treaty; Borah Acting In Accord

Zeppelin Lands In Brazil, Completing Ocean Flight Of 4,000 Miles In 61 Hours

Avalanche Engulfs Party On Kanchenjunga Climb; Porter Is Killed, 2 Hurt

Duce's Hearers Cry 'Down With France!'

Hoover Hurries To Capital And Settles Tariff Snarl; Flexible Plan Agreed On

Buyer Of Liquor Commits No Crime, The Supreme Court Rules In Test Case; Modified Jones Law Reported To House

Tariff Bill In Jeopardy As Curtis Ruling Sends It Back To Conference

Fort Now Declares Homes Cannot Brew Intoxicating Drinks

Flexible Tariff Revised; New Power For President But He Cannot Cut Rates

President At Gettysburg Extols Lincoln's Ideals As Guide For Nation Now

JUNE

Zeppelin Lands After Battling Squalls, Covering 13,400 Miles In 204 1/2 Hours; Fuels To Fly Home At 10 P.M. Tomorrow

Islip Asylum Fire, Fourth In A Year, Injures 3 Seriously

Zeppelin Off For Home, Circles Over New York; Fair Weather On Course

Cannon Refuses To Tell Senators Of War On Smith; Warned Of 'Consequences'

Cannon Gives Fund Data To Press After Defying Senate Committee Again

Mercury Again At 90; Two Die, Ten Felled

Rockefeller Offers City 56-Acre $13,000,000 Park To Include Art Museum

Carol Will Be King Today By Vote Of Parliament; Rumanian Cabinet Resigns

Carol Proclaimed King Amid Rumania's Cheers; Coronation In October

Simon Report Reaffirms Goal Of Indian Self-Rule, But People Must Reform

Senate To Vote On Tariff Friday, House Saturday; Bankers' Head Hits Bill

Liners's Captain Accused After Sinking Of Tanker; 48 Died In Fire Or Sea

Reed And Grundy Assail But Accept Tariff Bill; Passage Is Now Expected

Senate Passes Tariff Bill By 44 To 42; Five Democrats Help 'Regulars' To Win; Europe Takes First Move In Reprisal

House Passes Tariff Bill 222-153, Ending Long Fight; Hoover Expected To Sign

Hoover Said He Will Sign The Tariff Bill; Hails Flexible Clause As Giving Power To Correct Faults, End Foreign Protests

Democrats Turn Tariff Fire On Hoover As Senate Sends Bill To White House; Break In Stock And Commodity Prices

Hoover Signs Tariff Bill As Borah In Senate Seeks Cuts By Flexible Clause

City Welcomes Admiral Byrd Today; Marine Pageant And Parade To Greet Him After Two Years In Antarctic

Byrd And His Men Acclaimed By City; Wildly Cheered In Broadway Parade; Walker Bestows Medals Of Merit

Six Climb Jonsong Peak, 24,340 Feet In Himalayas; Highest Scaled By Man

Virginians Acclaim Byrd In Gala Fete In Richmond; State Gives Him A Sword

Son Born to Col. And Mrs. Lindbergh On the 24th Birthday of the Mother

Kingsford-Smith Hops From Ireland With 3 Aides For Non-Stop Flight Here; He Radioes 'All O.K.' 4 1-2 Hours Out

Kingsford-Smith Crosses The Atlantic Ocean; May Land In Newfoundland Or Nova Scotia; Messages Direct To The Times Tell Of Flight

Kingsford-Smith Flying To New York From Harbor Grace; Due About 4 P.M.; His Own Story Of Fighting Fog At Sea

Ocean Fliers Land At Roosevelt Field After Circling City; 10,000 Rush Plane; Kingsford-Smith Tells Flight Details

10,000 At City Hall Hail Ocean Fliers, Mayor Decorates Them, Lauds Daring; Leader Writes Of Compass Mystery

Rhineland Regains Freedom Tomorrow

Williams Flies To Bermuda And Back, Making Non-Stop Dash In 17 Hours; Endurance Fliers Set Record, Keep On

JULY

Campbell, Out, Charges Deals In Liquor Permits To Aid State Republicans

M'Campbell Makes 7 Raids, Opening Drive To Dry City; House Inquiry Here Urged

New Clue To Cyclops' Loss, Telling Of Dynamite Plot, May Solve War Mystery

Congress Adjourns With Hoover Victor On Law Board Fund And Veterans' Bill; Senate Bows To The House Amendments

Endurance Fliers Forced To Quit After Setting Record At 553 Hours; Break In Oil Gauge Upsets Plans

Nation's Death Rate Halved Since 1900; Diphtheria Cut 95%

Senate Convenes Today But Faces Lack Of Quorum; Treaty Action Tomorrow

Hoover Message Opens Treaty Fight; Opposition Calls For Secret Documents; 58 Senators Sit In Special Session

Fight Over Treaty Papers Occupies Senate Session; Swanson Pleads For Pact

Senate Wrangles 5 Hours On Secret Treaty Papers; No Vote On Them In Sight

Senate, 53-4, Asks Hoover For Secret Treaty Data, But On His Own Terms

Hoover Refuses Pact Data And 2 Senators Join Foes; Norris Moves Reservation

Hoover Confers At Camp To Speed Treaty Action; Loss Of Quorum Feared

Treaty Forces To Seek Ratification In Ten Days; Plan Mapped With Hoover

Ewald Quits The Bench; Now Faces State Charge Of Falsifying His Records

'Secret Navy Plan' Produced By Reed; Virtually Same As Draft Made Public; 'Freedom Of Seas' Reservation Planned

Red Riots in Shanghai Result in Martial Law; Communists Stone Cars as Civil War Protest

Treaty Backers To Force Continuous Session If Foes Do Not Agree To Cut Debate

Walker Orders An Inquiry On Graft In City Bureaus; Gives Higgins Wide Power

100 Hurt In P.R.R. Wreck; Coaches Leap Off Trestle Into Street At Elizabeth

Roosevelt Rejects Plea For City Inquiry Session; Demands More Evidence

Senate Ratifies Naval Treaty, 58-9; Only Norris Reservation Is Accepted; Extra Session Then Quickly Adjourns

President Signs Treaty; Calls Our Action A Move To Renew 'World Faith'

679 Killed In Italian Earthquake; Injured Put At 1,500; Relief Rushed; Naples In Terror As Houses Crumble

Quake Deaths Put Officially At 2,000, But May Exceed 2,500; 10,000 Injured; Italian Nation Mobilised For Relief

Five New Quakes In Italy, Razing Weakened Houses; Known Dead Put At 1,883

Einstein Evolving Yet Another Theory

Heat Of 89 Kills 6; 12 Bathers Drown

Canada Goes Conservative; Liberals Beaten On Tariff; We Face Big Trade Loss

Hoover Opposes Barring Soviet Trade In General; Ban On Convict Goods Only

R-100 Plows Through Fog Over The Coast Of Canada; Due To Land Late Today

AUGUST

R-100 Arrives At Montreal Airport; Battles Storm As She Nears Her Goal; Damaged Fin Repaired As Ship Drifts

R-100 Was Near Disaster; Shot Skyward 2,500 Feet By Storm Over Quebec

5 Big Oil Companies To Sell Auto Tires At Service Stations

Roosevelt Attacks Rise By 1,000,000 Small Users By Electric Meter Levy

Farmers Ask Hoover's Aid To Meet Drought Menace; 90-Degree Heat Here, 3 Die

Hoover Takes Up Drought Relief Plans; Says He Will 'Leave No Stone Unturned'; Two Die Here As Record Heat Persists

Walker Suspends Healy For Silence On Charge Ewald Bought Bench Job

Mayor's $228,000,000 Price For B.M.T. Brings Deadlock; $160,000,000 Urged By Board

Hoover To Call 12 Governors To Confer On Drought Relief, Bets Hyde Survey; 1,000,000 Farm Families Are Affected

Rail Rates Cut For Drought Relief; Hoover At Rapidan Camp Speeds Plans; Red Cross Mobilizes All Chapters

Hoover Perfects Plans For Drought Relief Body; States To Name Members

Drought Cut In Corn Crop Put At 690,000,000 Bushels; Food Shortage In 2 States

Mayor Denies $10,000 Got Ewald His Job, Or That Healy Was Consulted About It; Olvany Backs

Hawks Flies From Coast In 12 1/2 Hours, 2 1/2 Under Mark Set By The Lindberghs; Exceeds 200-Mile Speed All The Way

Nine-Point Program For Drought Relief Adopted By President And Governors; Widespread Rains Break Dry Spell

Governor Calls For All The Records In Ewald Case When Dr Wise Protests; Healy Had $10,000 When He Got Loan

Freak Hail Storm Hits City, Batters New England Crops

Mysery Plane Built for 300 Miles an Hour Flashes Over Course Here in Racing Test

Racketeers Keep City Food Prices High, Witnesses Reveal At State Inquiries; Death Threats And Sabotage Charged

Van Lear Black Missing From Yacht Off Jersey; Wide Hunt By Air And Sea

Governor Maps Wide City Bench Inquiry; Formal Announcement Expected Today; Healy Quits As Ward Gets Crain Data

Governor Asks City Bench Inquiry By Appellate Court, But Limits Ward; Baldwin Seeks Action Against Walker

Bodies Of Airmen Lost 33 Years Found Near Where Balloon Fell In Arctic; Andree And Comrades Frozen At Camp

Warship To Bring Andree's Body Back; He Had Neared Pole

Appellate Justices Act Today On Inquiry Into Magistrates

Cash Says He Paid Healy $2,000 For Marshal's Job; Inquiry On Bench Decided

German Fliers Alight At The Battery; Hailed By City For Crossing Atlantic By Way Of Greenland In 47 Hours' Flying

Mayor Admits Widespread Petty Graft; Asks Civic Groups To Help Wipe It Out; Critics See Evasion Of Blame For Evils

Guns Guard Buenos Aires; Troops Protect Irigoyen; Revolution Plot Mooted

Thinks Andree Lived Two Years In Arctic

Ward Consults Bar On Widening Scope Of Ewald Inquiry

SEPTEMBER

Find Treasure Ship With Lost $5,000,000 400 Feet Under Sea

Andree And Aides Died Of Exhaustion; Bodies Found Are Mere Skeletons; Identified By Labels On Equipment

Coste Does It In 37 Hours, 18 1/2 Minutes! First To Make Paris-New York Flight; Hoover, Lindbergh And Byrd Hail Feat

City Greets Fliers In Gay Pageant; Gets Medals; Off For Dallas At 6 A.M.; Good-Will Tour Of Nation Planned

Santo Domingo Wrecked By Hurricane; 800 Dead, Hundreds Hurt In City Alone; Washington Rushing Relief To Island

Hurricane Toll Now 1,200; Dominicans Burning Dead To Save City From Plague

Revolution Triumphs In Argentina; Junta Assumes Power As Troops Oust Irigoyen's Regime And Arrest Him

Argentine Revolt Sweeps The Nation; Army Men Replace State Governors; Martial Law Curbs buenos Aires Mobs

Counter-Revolt In Buenos Aires Mars The Inauguration Of General Uriburu; Irigoyen And His Aides Are Arrested

Argentina Quells Riots; President Uriburu To Ask Prompt Recognition Here

Uriburu Talks To Times In A Wireless Interview; Requests Our Friendship

Briand And Henderson Clash At Geneva; Latter Demands Disarmament At Once; Former Asks Federation For Security

Columbus in America Before 1492, But Via Greenland, Savant Finds

Enterprise Victor In First Cup Race, Leading The Shamrock All The Way; Gay Newport Is A Colorful Setting

Fascists Make Big Gains In Germany, Communists Also Increase Strength As Moderates Drop In Reich Election

Justice M'Cook Allows Full Job-Buying Inquiry By The Ewald Grand Jury

Tuttle Sends Hoover Resignation, And Declares For Dry Law Repeal; Wets Fail To Gain In State Primaries

Capital Sees Big Wet Gain In Primaries With Unrest Aiding In Upsets Of Drys; Leaders In Quandary On Tuttle Stand

Enterprise Wins Series And American Keeps Cup; His Last Try, Says Lipton

Ewald And Wife Indicted With Healy And Tommaney On Office-Buying Charge

Roosevelt Men Expect Close Race, Due To Scandals

Hoover Men Move To Bar Repeal In State Platform; Wets Ask Official Dictum

Soviet Undersells Our Wheat Abroad; Report Of 10-Cent Cut Halts Export; Chicago Pit Asks Hyde For Full Facts

Tuttle Insists On Repeal In Final Word To Albany; Hopes Of The Wets Rise

Nomination Of Tuttle By Republicans On Repeal Platform Appears Certain; Drys May Run Independent Candidate

Republicans Agree On Repeal Plank; Tuttle On First Ballot Is The Forecast; Stimson, As Keynoter, Omits Dry Issue

Tuttle Nominated On Wet Platform; Makes Tammany Defiance The Issue; Repeal Plank Is Adopted, 733 To 258

Dictatorship For Germany, With Hindenburg At Head, Bruening's Threat To Foes

Roosevelt Demands Tammany Testify, In Letter To Walker Scoring Immunity; Mayor To Tell District Chiefs To Do So

Democrats Adopt Straight Wet Plank And Bar Immunity Pleas In Platform; Curry Ends Aides' Revolt On Testifying

OCTOBER

Roosevelt Nominated By Acclamation, Challenges Tuttle On State Dry Law; Smith Says Party Will Oust Grafters

Waive Immunity Or Go, Walker Tells His Aides; Gives Them Day To Decide

Hoover Asks Bankers to Take Lead In A Speedy Revival Of Prosperity; Upholds Our High Standard Of Living

Governor, Accepting, Calls Tuttle Both Wet And Dry; Charges Hoover Influence

British Airship R-101 Is Destroyed In Crash And Explosion In France; 46 Aboard Perish, 7 Badly Injured

Weight Of Rain Forced Down R-101; Dipped Twice, Hit Hill, Then Burned; Survivors Battled Through Flames

80,000 Rebels Move On Rio And Sao Paulo From South; Long Struggle Forecast

Hoover Warns Of Perils Of Red Doctrines In Talk To Kings Mountain

Judge Bertini Refuses To Testify; Roosevelt Asks Senate To Be Ready To Take Quick Action On His Removal

Governor Tells How Crater And Bertini Were Appointed By Him To The Bench; Ward Resents Roosevelt Jury Move

Britain To Reject Demand Of Dominions On Tariff; For Bulk Buying Instead

3 Indictments Likely In Bertini Case; Todd, Tracing $100,000 Funds, Studies Bank Records Of Judge And Kohler

Jack Diamond Shot 5 Times By Gunmen In A 64th St. Hotel

Governor Criticizes Ward, Insisting On Bertini Data; $30,000 Reported Traced

Flynn Is Questioned On Bronx Judgeship; Roosevelt Plea Up

First Uncensored News From Brazil's Loyal Area Reveals Grave Situation

Reds Invade City Hall; Heckle Mayor And Fight Police, Who Hold Sixteen

President Acts To Spur Employment, Naming Cabinet Board To Devise Plans; City Votes $1,000,000 To Aid Jobless

Bruening Is Victor In Reichstag Voting; Disorders Continue

Up-State Fails To Show Big Registration Gain; Apathy In Dry Counties

Roosevelt Assails Hoover 'Prosperity': Hit's Inflation Orgy'

Tammany Combats Corruption Charge; Smith And Walker Uphold City Regime As Tuttle Presses Graft Issue Here

Trade Revival On Big Scale Predicted By Business Leaders Meeting In Chicago; Plans For Relief Of Idle Here Speeded

Government And Industry To Create Jobs For Idle; City To Feed 12,000 Daily

Revolution Triumphs In All Brazil; President Prisoner, Prestes In Hiding; Rioting In Rio; Sao Paulo Joins In Coup

Brazil Now Faces Fight For Control; Anarchists Loot And Burn In Sao Paulo

Vargas Takes Presidency Of Brazil In Rio Today; Order Restored In Nation

Roosevelt Replies On Corruption; Scores 'Loose' Charges Of City Graft; Tuttle Denies Dodging On Liquor Issue

Stimson Urges Election Of Tuttle For Clean-Up; Calls Roosevelt 'Unfit'

Roosevelt Denounces 'Whisperers'; Says 'Half Truths' Will Defeat Rivals; Tuttle Charges Governor Is 'Bluffing'

Earthquake Wrecks Wide Area In Italy, Centring On Ancona

NOVEMBER

Roosevelt Scores Attack By Stimson As 'Hypocrisy': Purge Bench, Tuttle Urges

Convict Slain, 3 Wounded As Four Men Try To Shoot Their Way Out Of Sing Sing

Germany Seeks Showdown On Disarming 'Hypocrisy'; Won't Stay Unarmed Alone

Final Roosevelt Plea On State Issues; Tuttle Stresses Need For Honest Rule; Both Major Parties See Victory Today

Democratic Landslide Sweeps Country; Republicans May Lose Congress Control; Roosevelt Winner By More Than 700,000

Republicans Lose Grip On Congress; Insurgents Hold Balance Of Power; Wets Have 134 In House, 18 In Senate

Bloc Control Likely In New Congress; Republicans Cannot Get House Majority; Can Organize Senate By Farm-Labor Aid

Democrats Pledge Business Their Aid And Offer Cooperation With President; House Republican By 1 On Latest Count

Hoover Plans More Jobs For The Idle; Will Ask Congress To Provide Funds; Seed Loan For Farmers Proposed, Too

Offer Of Democratic Aid In Ending Slump Accepted After White House Parley

1.7% Decline In Jobs Spurs Relief Groups To Rush Aid For Idle

Hoover Hits At Wider Kellogg Pact In Armistice Day Plea To Guard Peace; Again Calls For Entry In World Court

Hoover Asks Democrats To Aid Congress Program, Averting Special Session

Hoover Announces Truce By Rival Senate Leaders; Now Fears No Filibuster

Priest Is Beheaded By Chinese Bandits; 4 In Mission Seized

Rioters Terrorize Madrid; Revolt Brewing In North; Troops Are Ready To Act

Governor Plans Loan Funds For Idle Through His Board

Roosevelt Will Invite Six Governors To Confer On The Jobless Problem

$1,400,000 Raised In Drive To Provide Jobs For Idle; Harkness Gives $500,000

Hoover Calls Upon Nation To Give Child 'Fair Chance' In Stress Of Gruelling Era

Wide Federal Drive On Racketeers; New York And Other Cities To Get Aid; $5,000,000 Fund Backs Chicago's War

Grip Of Rackets On City Bared In Fifty Complaints; Vast Toll Exacted Yearly

Threat Of Dry Party If Hoover Is 'Moist'

Way Opened For France To Ask Hoover To Implement Kellogg Anti-War Pact; Geneva Expects Paris To Act Quickly

Got $20,000 To Free 900 In Vice Cases, Prosecutor Confesses, Exposing Ring

Silbermann Used Bench To Aid Friends, 2 Swear; Girl Tells Of 'Frame-Up'

28 Policemen Named As Vice Grafters; Informers Admits Aiding 150 Frame-Ups; Walker And Mulrooney Act Quickly

Quick Action By Governor Demanded In Vice Expose; Jury Disagrees On Healy

President Will Submit World Court For Senate Action In This Congress; Opposition Rises, Extra Session Looms

Long World Court Fight Now Considered Likely, Upsetting Congress Plans

DECEMBER

Stalin Sees Capitalists Drifting Surely To War; Puzzled By Our Attitude

Congress Truce To Help Business Indicated As Short Session Opens; Tear Gas Drives Reds From Capitol

Hoover Asks $150,000,000 To Aid Idle; Warns Of Deficit And End Of Tax Cut; His Control Of Works Fund Opposed

Hoover Urges Congress To Economize As He Presents Record Peace Budget; 4,860,000 Idle In Nation, Green Says

Hoover Lists Public Works Projects, Urging Congress To Speed $150,000,000; $8,000,000 New Goal Of Job Fund Here

Scores Die, 300 Stricken By Poison Fog In Belgium; Panic Grips Countryside

Hoover Asks Congress Aid To Avert A Tax Increase; House Bill Cuts Job Fund

4 Escaped Maniacs Seized In Brooklyn By Lone Detective

First Relief Bills Ready, But Walsh Hits Program; Hyde Warns Against Dole

Hoover Lays Flood Of Job Measures To Politics And Senators Attack Him; $170,000,000 Relief Bills Advanced

Robinson Asks Cooperation On Relief, But He Condemns
President's Criticism; Hoover Submits World Court Protocol

Bank Of U.S. Closes Doors; State Takes Over Affairs; Aid Offered
To Depositors

Revolt Starts In Spain; Rebels Take Border City And Advance On
Another

Einstein Receives 'Keys' to The City

Forty Detectives Accused As Criminal Court 'Fixers' Operating
With Lawyers

Madrid Air Force's Revolt Crushed by Artillery Fire; Spain Under
Martial Law

Federal Judge Holds Prohibition Void; Finds Method Of Its
Adoption Illegal; Ruling In New Jersey Stirs Washington

Mitchell Hastens Appeal On New Jersey Wet Ruling; Dry Raids
Will Continue

Congress Conferees Agree On $45,000,000 Drought Aid; Hoover
Wins Senate Fight

Stalin Dismisses Rykoff As Soviet Prime Minister; Dictator Is Now
Supreme

Hoover Victor As Congress Adjourns; His Relief Measures Passed
And Signed; All Power Board Nominees Confirmed

High Tammany Men Named By Kresel In Inquiry On Funds

NYE Bares $40,000 Republican Fund As Linked To Lucas's Fight
On Norris; Party Crisis Over Insurgents Forseen

Republican Leader Visits Hoover, Then Backs Lucas; 'Party Plot,' Says Norris

All Needy To Share City's Feast Today In Record Charity

Dewey Asks Norris To Lead New Party; Lucas Row Is Cited

Norris Declines To Head New Party; Still A Republican

Crain Acts On Bank Of U.S.; Calls Grand Jury Inquiry; State Also To Seek Fraud

$489,804,000 Price Set For B.M.T. And I.R.T. By Untermyer For A Unified System With 5-Cent Fare; Dahl Accepts Figure

Seabury Inquiry 'Illegal,' City's Counsel Charges; Corrigan Shifts 150 Aides

Court Inquiry Will Go On, Governor Says, Promising New Legislation If Needed; Knight Pledges Aid Of The Republicans

1931: NEW YORK TIMES (365)

JANUARY

Hoover To Act As Arbiter In Rail Grouping Dispute; Couzens
Assails His Stand

8 American Marines Slain In Nicaraguan Ambush Led By Aide Of
Sandino

Quick Revolt In Panama Overturns Government; President Goes
To Exile

City-Wide Inquiry Mapped By Republicans At Albany; Governor
To Get Measure

$171,547,000 Project To Dam St. Lawrence Submitted To State

Roosevelt Calls On Crain To Prosecute Vigorously His Bank Of
U.S. Inquiry

Goodman Quits Under Fire; Court Suspends Brodsky; Rothstein's
Loans Sifted

Governor, In Message, Puts City Inquiry Up To Legislature; Will
Approve Funds; Broderick Asks Drastic Bank Reforms

Pope Pius XI, In Encyclical, Condemns Trial Marriage, Divorce
And Birth Control

Silbermann Assailed On Three Verdicts, One The Jailing Of Sister
Of Two Priests; May Bespeaks Aid To Wipe Out Abuses

Hoover Rebukes Senate On Power Board; Refuses To Return Names Of 3 Nominees; Senators, 36 To 23, Accept His Challenge

Wiggins Advises U.S. To Cut War Debts To Aid Trade; Calls Our Tariff Too High

Governor Asks $48,000,000 to Make Jobs By Speeding Action On Public Works; Republicans Act To Widen City Inquiry

Geneva Sees Reform Imperative To Save World's Gold Basis

Jailed Minor Girls To Get New Trials By Bennett Order

Woman Of Standing Framed In Vice Case, Jailed For Ten Days

Simpson Quits Bench As He Faces Inquiry; Mayor Ends Leaves

Fish Report Asks Outlawing Of Reds As National Menace

President Names Coolidge And Smith To Head Red Cross Relief Fund Drive; Senate Insists On Its Own $25,000,000

Senate Defies President, Voting $25,000,000 Again; His Relief Policy Scored

Wickersham Report Opposes Repeal, But Board Majority Favors Revision; Hoover Is Firm For Dry Enforcement

Senate Inquiry On Dry Report Sought; Commission Denies Hoover Influence; President's Mind Is 'Open' On Revision

Director Admits He Lost $250,000 Bank Of U.S. Loan Gambling In Stock Market

Governors Advised To Fight Idleness With Job Insurance

Mysterious $65,000 Traced To 2 Police At 'Fixer' Hearing

Release Of Gandhi Ordered By Viceroy; Congress Ban Lifted

M'Donald Triumphs In Debate On India As Gandhi Goes Free

Boy Prisoners Riot, Fell Jersey Guards; 9 Wounded, 9 Escape

$25,000,000 Drought Fund Is Declined By Red Cross; Senators Assail Hoover

United States Apologizes To Mussolini; General Butler To Be Court-Martialed For Slur On Italian Premier In Speech

Senate Democrats End Congress Truce As House Kills $25,000,000 For Relief; Demand Drought Fund Or Extra Session

FEBRUARY

House Committee To Press Embargo On Soviet Products

$75,000,000 In Bank Of U.S. Lost, In Doubt Or 'Frozen';
Broderick Files Inventory

Kresel Defends Bank Of U.S. Practices, Denies Steuer Charge Of
Irregularity; Bar Inquiry Asked On Levy's Rulings

Steuer Charges Graft In Deals Of Bank Of U.S.; Marcus Assails
Mitchell

Illegal Loans To Officers Charged As Grand Jurors Hear Bank Of
U.S. Chairman

Kresel Denies Liability For Affiliates As Steuer Calls Bank Deals
Crooked

Hoover And Senators End Deadlock; They Agree On $20,000,000
Relief Fund Available For Loans In Drought Area

Amelia Earheart Weds G.P. Putnam

Gen. Butler Freed With A Reprimand As He Voices Regret

Indictment Of 7 In Bank Of U.S. Voted; Kresel Leaves Sickbed To
Testify; Singer Says He Lost Entire Fortune

Kresel, Indicted With 7 In Bank Of U.S., Quits As Prosecutor In Court Inquiry; Steuer Halted; Bank Records Burned

World Parley On Silver And Loan To Revive China Urged In Senate Report

Pope Speaks to World In Greatest Broadcast; Message Stresses Peace

Lt. Kenna Banked $237,235, Police 'Higher-Ups' Sought; Jean Norris 'Fixed' Record

$20,000,000 Drought Aid Bill Made Law As Congress Passes And Hoover Signs It; Borah Leads Last Stand Of Senate Foes

British 5-Year Plan Is Proposed To Save Nation's Industries

$400,000 Speakeasy Graft From 125 Resorts Is Laid To 2 Police 'Collectors'

51 Police Bank Accounts Subpoenaed In Wide Hunt For 'Higher-Ups' In Graft

City Inquiry Is Defeated; Later Shifts Of Ward Men Opens Way For New Vote

Senate Votes Bonus Loan Bill, 72 To 12; President Says He Will Veto It At Once; Both Houses Prepared To Override Him

Congress Is Asked To Curb Rail Holding Companies, Placing Them Under I.C.C.

60 Shot As Radicals Fight Cuban Police

White Man Crosses The Arabian Desert For The First Time

24 Nations Gather To Shape Grain Plan For The Old World

Six Bank Of U.S. Heads Seek To Throw Out Indictments; Charge Jurors Own Stock

Thomas Tells His Story Of Arabian Desert Trek; Found 7-Mile Salt Lake

Woman Vice Case Witness Found Strangled In Park; Her Lawyer Is Arrested

Two Held In $100,000 Bail In Gordon Murder Case; She Charged Police Plot

MARCH

Rome Joins Naval Accord, Ends Rivalry With Paris; To Complete 5-Power Pact

Policeman And Ex-Husband Deny Framing Miss Gordon; Grand Jury To Hear Them

Miss Gordon's Diary Says Three Sought To Kill Her; Vice Ring Theory Dropped

Laxity Laid To Broderick As He Admits Bank Of U.S. Made 'Dishonest' Deals

$10,000,000,000 Congress Quits, Vital Bills Lost By Filibuster In Senate

Raskob Proposal For State Liquor Rule Starts A Storm In National Committee; Robinson Attacks, Smith Defends Him

Ruth Nichols Soars Six Miles Above City, Setting New Record

Roosevelt Orders Inquiry On Crain After City Club Demands His Removal For Misfeasance In Prosecuting Graft

Way Opened For Sweeping City Inquiry; Roosevelt, Defying Tammany, Names Seabury To Hear Crain Ouster Charges

Seabury Accepts, To Speed Impartial Inquiry On Crain; Tammany Hall Resentful

Demand For Walker Inquiry Drawn; Inaction In City Corruption
Charged; Prosecutor's Gordon Case Data Gone

Demand For City-Wide Inquiry Grows; Crain Asks Untermyer To
Aid His Fight; Tammany Sees Roosevelt As Accuser

Federated Churches Ask Wide Inquiry; Formal Charges Against
Mayor Ready; Governor Would Let Legislature Act

Crain Protests Inquiry By Seabury, Alleging Bias; Walker Charges
Pressed

Untermyer Will Act As Crain's Counsel; Kerrigan Sees Plot To End
Bank Expose; Governor To Continue Seabury's Power

Mayor To Answer Critics; Calls Inquiry 'Nonsense'; Aide Offers To
Prove Plot

20 Killed, Scores Hurt, As Ship Blows Up; Movie Men On Sealer
Among Missing; Sixty Reach Island Off Newfoundland

24 Missing From The Viking; Sargeant, Injured, Is Saved; Rescue
Boats Reach Island

Laxity In Ten Scandals Laid To Walker; Charges Are Made Public
By Roosevelt, Who Bans Speculation On His Decision

Seabury Puts Curb On Crain's Counsel; Roosevelt May Ask Walker
Defense; Four Vice Squad Policemen Indicted

Buckner Link In Crain Case Led To Bank Plot Charge; Mayor
Relies On Governor

Germany And Austria Join In A Full Customs Union; Evasion Of
Treaties Seen

3 Nations Warn Austria On Deal With Germany; She Presses Tariff Union

Legislature Votes Inquiry Into City With Ward Aid And Seabury In Charge; Governor Mails Accusations To Mayor

Tammany, Stunned, Plans To Fight Back; Seabury To Get A Free Hand In Inquiry; Roosevelt Won't Shirk Walker Ruling

Britain Demands Review Of Trade Pact By League; Reich Refuses To Yield

Bastress Arrested On Bribery Charge, First In Tammany's Move For Clean-Up; More Resignations Are Now Forecast

Gandhi Triumphant At Indian Congress; Will Go To London

Von Hindenburg To Rule; Puts Curb On Civil Rights To End Political Violence

Mayor Plans Shake-Up Of Two Bureaus; Republicans Act To Bar His Transit Rule; Seabury And Macy To Map Inquiry Today

Mass Meeting Denounces Walker And His Regime; Ousting In 100 Days Seen

APRIL

Managua Is Destroyed, 1,100 Reported Killed, Thousands Injured In Earthquake And Fire; Many American Casualties; Hoover Rushes Aid

25,000 Homeless Flee Managua Ruins; City May Be Abandoned As Capital; Medical Supplies Arrive By Plane

Quake Toll Rises To 2,000; 500 Dead Found At Market; Relief Reaching Managua

Racket Clean-Up On; $200,000,000 Tribute Paid Yearly In City

Walker, Returning Today, Warns Aids They Must Testify Or Lose Their Jobs; Magistrates Face Federal Tax Action

Mayor Walker Returns; Takes Up Defense Today; Job-Buying Inquiry Fails

Aides Give Mayor Data To Fight Ouster Charges; Tammany More Confident

Crain Hearing Opens Today; City Inquiry Board Named; Vice Policeman Sentenced

Couldn't Stop Rackets, Crain Admits; He Ignored Evidence, Clark Charges; Seabury Asks $500,000 For Inquiry

Seabury Piles Up Evidence Of A Vast Market Racket, Rebukes Crain's Counsel

Crain Opens His Defense; Lacked Power, Says Aide, To Drive Out Racketeers

Mulrooney Replaces Entire Vice Squad; A New General Order Bars Informers To Cure Abuses Revealed By Seabury

Republicans Sweep Polls In Most Of Spanish Cities; New Perils Loom For King

Foes Demand Alfonso Quit Or Face Republic By Force; Spanish Cabinet To Resign

King Alfonso Quits, Spain A Republic; Alcala Zamora Is First President; Nation Orderly Under Martial Law

Spain Proclaims New Bill Of Rights; Zamora Asks Powers For Confidence; King On Cruiser Reaches Marseilles

Paris Cheers King Alfonso As He Joins Queen In Exile; Spain Goes Back To Work

Washington Withdraws Its Protection From Americans In Central Nicaragua; Citizens Of Other Countries Affected

Stimson Defends Change In His Nicaraguan Policy; Disturbed By Opposition

Revolution In Honduras; Our Warships Rush There As Rebels Capture Town

Walker, In Reply, Calls Charges False; Cites His Reforms And Scores Critics; Roosevelt Silent, Defers His Decision

Accusers Ask Open Trial Of Walker, With Roosevelt Presiding In Person; Republicans Repudiate Fox's Attack

Seabury Demands Record Of All Higgins's Inquiries; Blow At Walker Is Seen

Washburn Accuses Crain Of Blocking $100,000,000 Stock Frauds Fight In 1930; Prosecutor 'Unsuspicious' Of Vice Ring

Pope Quits Vatican To Honor Americans For Aiding College

Tammany's Chiefs Confer On Strategy; Curry Denies Advising Inquiry Be Defied

Walker Sees A Red Plot Behind Move To Oust Him; Tammany To Test Inquiry

Clean-Up Of Diamond Gang Ordered By The Governor; Wounded Leader Is Dying

Governor Dismisses Walker Charges; Accusers To Carry On Removal Fight; Score Ruling That Complaint Is Vague

City Investigators Hail Walker Rulings; Tammany Is Irked

MAY

Crain Worst Prosecutor In 25 Years, Moley Shows By Review Of Records

Empire State Tower, Tallest In World, Is Opened By Hoover

George F. Baker, 91, Dies Suddenly Of Pneumonia; Dean Of Nation's Bankers

Ahrenberg Reaches Greenland In Plane To Save Courtauld

Hoover Urges Arms Cut To Revive Trade In Opening World Chamber Of Commerce; Foreign Delegates Attack High Tariffs

World Chamber Takes Up War Debts, Called Bar To Trade; Furor On Silver; Keep Living Standard, Mellon Urges

United Action By Nations To Start Business Moving Urged On World Chamber

Police Slayer Captured In Gun And Tear Gas Siege; 10,000 Watch In W. 90th St.

World Chamber Leaders Move For An Agreement On War Debts And Tariff

Wegener Given Up As Lost In Greenland's Ice Fields; Three Aides Found Safe

Revolt Seen Near To Unseat Uriburu; Argentina Is Tense

Riots In 7 Spanish Cities; Churches Looted, Burned; Martial Law Is Declared

Move To Try Alfonso For Spanish Riots; Army Forces Order

Wegener Gave Up His Life To Save Greenland Aides; Left So Food Would Last

Tammany Is Over-Ridden In Fight On City Inquiry; Seabury Program Upheld

Pope Demands Justice For Workers, With Fairer Distribution Of Wealth; Scores Communism, Calls For Harmony

French And Germans Clash At Geneva; Customs Pact Is Injected Into Debate; Wheat Parley To Seek Curb On Exports

Decision By World Court Sought On Customs Union; French Call Pact Illegal

World Court And League Will Settle Customs Dispute With German Consent; Russia Offers An Economic Peace Pact

League Launches Action To End World Depression; Henderson Hits Tariffs

America Bars Wheat Pool Which All Others Accept; Parley Failure Is Feared

Soviet Demands Right To Dump Wheat At Will; Moves Deadlocks Parley

Millikan Hails Radio As Leading Mankind To Democratic Ideal

Great Air Armada Thrills Millions; Makes 160-Mile Circle Without Mishap; New York Dedicates Municipal Airport

Confession Names Stein As Slayer Of Vivian Gordon

Witnesses Hidden, Two Indictments In Gordon Murder

Seven Are Lost On Cruise Of College Group In Sound; One Body Washed Ashore

Piccard Balloon Drifts Helplessly Above Alps; Scientists Feared Dead

Piccard Is Safe In Tyrol; Balloon Lands On Glacier After Rise Of 52,462 Feet

Piccard Tells His Story Of Trip To Stratosphere; Escaped Death Narrowly

Mussolini Suspends Catholic Action; K. Of C. Grounds Shut; Vatican Guarded; Pius XI Cancels Eucharistic Congress

JUNE

Pius XI Charges Fascisti With Hate And Violence; Four Bombings In Bologna

Mussolini Now Bans Catholic Societies Of Boys And Girls

Pinchot Attacks Utilities For 'Graft'; Urges Federal Rule Before Governors; Roosevelt Hits 'Passive' Government

Mussolini Orders Drive On All Foes Of Fascism; Catholic Leaders Jailed

German Revolution Is Feared In Geneva

Lindbergh Drafting Rout East Over Arctic To China Via Greenland And Siberia

Germany Presses Debt Cuts In Britain; Decree Says She Is End Of Resources; Borah Favors Revision Of Reparations

Move For International Aid Forecast As Germans End Conference In Britain; Change Seen In Our Attitude On Debts

Hoover's Debt Cut Hint Held Definite Proposal; Arms Reduction Awaited

Italy Answers Pope, Charging Bad Faith; Truce Held Certain

Starr Faithfull Beaten, Thrown Into Sea To Die, New Theory Of Edwards

Grand Jury Hears 15 Today In Murder Of Starr Faithfull

Indict Capone And 68 In Beer Conspiracy

$4,000,000 Payment Offered By Capone

350 Drowned Off France When Hurricane Capsizes Crowded Excursion Ship

Hoover Decries Depression Panaceas; Indianapolis Speech, Held Bid For 1932, Pictures Glowing Future For Nation

'Al' Capone Pleads Guilty To Charges; May Get 3 Years

Capone Conquered, Federal Men Come Here To Break Gangs

Industrial Success Emboldens Soviet In New World Policy

3 In Bank Of U.S. Guilty; Face Maximum Of 7 Years; Disagreement On Pollock

Hoover Proposes Year's War Debt Suspension With Moratorium For Germany On Reparations; European Capitals Hopeful; Stocks Rise Here

Berlin Officially Accepts Hoover Plan; London Willing, Paris To Ask Part Pay; President Got Data From Hindenburg

Debt Plan Wins French Popular Favor; Britain And Italy Give Full Support; Prices Rise In Markets Of The World

Post And Gatty Far Out At Sea On World Flight; Hillig And Hoiriis Follow

Post And Gatty Take Off For Moscow After Berlin Hails Them For Sea Hop; No Report Yet On Hillig And Hoiriis

Hoiriis And Hillig Safe At Bremen, Too Tired To Fly On To Danish Welcome; Post And Gatty Speeding On To Siberia

Post And Gatty Land Safely At Irkutsk; Copenhagen Acclaims Hoiriis And Hillig; Pilot's Own Story Of Flight To Denmark

French To Consult Germans On Debts As Mellon Wins Laval To Discussion Of Paris Reservation On Hoover Plan

Poles And Czechs Accept Hoover's War Debt Plan; Paris Talks To Continue

Post And Gatty Land Safely Near Nome After Hop Of 2,400 Miles From Siberia; Arrive Few Hours Later In Fairbanks

JULY

Post And Gatty Are Due Here Tonight; Reach Edmonton After 1,450-Mile Hop; City Prepares Big Welcome For Them

Post And Gatty End Their Record World Flight; Circled Globe In 8 Days, 15 Hours, 51 Minutes; 10,000 In Wild Demonstration At Field Here

Post And Gatty Get Stirring Welcome; Crowds Cheer World Fliers In Parade; Walker Decorates Them At City Hall

War Debt Accord Reached In Paris; Only Minor Details To Be Adjusted; Germany To Pay Basle, Then Get 'Loan'

'Basis Of Accord' Announced In Paris On Final Details Of Debt Holiday; Washington Thinks It Is Acceptable

Washington Sees Debt Accord Delay In Difference Over Payments In Kind, But Paris Expects Agreement Today

Final Agreement On Debts Is Signed In Paris; Payments Suspended For A Year From July 1; Hoover Plan Intact; All Capitalists Optimistic

London Summons Young Plan Powers To Settle Details of The Debt Accord; German Industry Pledges Big Credits

Reich To Seek Large Loan; Parley In London July 17; Italy Urges Arms Truce

Stimson Informed By Duce That Italy Wants Only Peace

Hoover Condemns Shorts Who Depress Grain Prices To Profit From Distress

Berlin Expects New York And London Will Help The Reichsbank Tomorrow To Prevent German Financial Crash

Federal Reserve Likely To Aid Reich In Cooperation With European Banks; Berlin Closes Boerses; Big Bank Fails

Central Banks Agree To Help Reich; Act After All-Day Meeting At Basle; German Bank Runs Bring 2-Day Closing

Germans Turn To Self Aid To End Crisis; Plan New Curbs, Longer Bank Closing; Further Central Bank Credit Doubted

Germany Curbs Exchange; Red Riots Quickly Ended; Powers To Meet Monday

Washington Joins Debt Conference, Taking New Role In World Politics; Paris And London Move To Aid Reich

Parleys On Reich Start In Paris Today, Germans Conferring With The French Before 5-Power Discussions Tomorrow

Progress Made In Franco-German Talk; French Decide To Go To London Parley; Washington Bars Loan Guarantee By US

France Agrees To Befriend Germany; Cordiality Marks Paris Conference; Seven Powers Meet In London Today

New Hoover Plan To Help Germany To Be Given To London Parley Today; Seven Powers Meet To Act On Crisis

Powers Agree To Base Aid For Reich On Hoover's New Credit
Proposal; Likely To Extend Short-Term Loans

Powers To Vote Aid To Reich Today, Taking Only Temporary Steps
Now; Wall Street Doubts Success Of Plan

Hoover Plan Voted by London Parley, Which Adjourns Amid
Felicitations; Efforts To Help Reich Will Continue

Hoover Bluntly Orders Slash In Budget Figures; Demands Action
By Aug. 17

Phone Call From Curry's Apartment Traced By Seabury To Lake
Placid, Where Judge Signed A Stay For Doyle

Revolt Wins In Chile As President Quits; Many Killed In Riots

Doyle Jailed As Appeal Is Denied Unanimously; Cardozo Gets New
Plea

Seabury Queries Olvany On His Bank Accounts; Doyle Must Stay
In Jail

Herndon, Pangborn Safe; Fog Stops Them In Wales; No Word Of
Other Plane

Boardman Plane Safe At Istanbul, Breaking World's Distance
Record; Herndon, Pangborn Go On To Moscow

AUGUST

Hoover Suggests Germany Buy Our Wheat And Cotton On Liberal Credit Terms

Thomas Edison Ill; Doctor Flies to Him

Lindberghs Speed North To Churchill; 2,000 Cheer Landing

Three Negroes Die In Chicago Red Riots

Troops Stop Flow Of Oklahoma Oil

Germany Calm As Banks Are Reopened; Day's Deposits Exceed Withdrawals; Bankers Here Agree On Credit Terms

Reich Offers To Buy Farm Board Cotton On Long-Term Credit

Dark Age Cruelty Charged In System For Deportations

Berlin Makes Offer To Buy 600,000 Tons Of American Wheat

Prussian Plebiscite Fails By 3,500,000; 13 Die In Berlin Riot

Special Legislative Session Forecast To Give Seabury Full Immunity Power; Appeals Court Upholds Doyle Jailing

Seabury To Examine Curry In Public Over Phone Call, Doyle Fights For Freedom

Cuban Rebellion Spreads As Thousands Join Ranks; 15 Are Killed
In Skirmish

Lindberghs To Fly Around The World After Hop To Japan

Curry Admits Phoning Judge Sherman; Calls Inquiry Crucifixion
Of Tammany; Doyle Out Today; Special Session Near

Legislature Meets Aug. 25 To Widen Immunity Power; Governor
Favors Measure

Wickersham Study Lays Rise In Crime To Unemployment

China Seeks To Buy Farm Board Wheat On Long-Term Loan

Tammany Men Rebuffed By Roosevelt On Fight For An Up-State
Inquiry

Cuban Rebels Defeated In Hard Battle At Jibara; Hundreds
Reported Slain

Fighting Begun In Havana And In Province Near City; Danish
Steamer Is Bombed

Great Yangtse Flood Engulfs Hankow; Hwai River Covers 80
Counties In North; Thousands Die, 30,000,000 Are Homeless

New War On Gangs Opened By City With Federal Aid; 3 Shot In
Street May Die

Three Lined Up And Shot Against Wall In Brooklyn By Gang
Execution Squad

M'Donald Heads Three-Party Cabinet To Put Through Program
Of Economy; New York And Paris Credits Assured

Governor Balks Tammany, Holding The Legislature To The Two Seabury Bills

Up-State Inquiry Likely; Tammany Presses Fight Against Seabury's Bills

Roosevelt Moves For Up-State Inquiry, Opening Way For Tammany's Charges; Both Houses Pass The Seabury Bills

Roosevelt Asks $20,000,000 For Jobless, Raising Fund By A 50% Income Tax Rise; Would Provide Work With 5-Day Week

Crain To Be Cleared But Scored As Lax In Seabury Report

200,000 More Dead Reported In China

SEPTEMBER

Governor Drops Charges Against Crain; Seabury Sustains 4 Of The 27 Counts But Holds His Removal Is Not Justified

Gov. Roosevelt Asks Firmer Laws To Aid Police War On Crime

King Of Yugoslavia Ends Dictatorship; New Charter Drawn

Berlin Stocks Fall 25 To 40 Per Cent As Boerse Reopens

$2,000,000,000 In Gold Finds 'Refuge' Here In Flight Of Capital

Roosevelt Demands War On Gangsters Throughout Nation

Chile Hears Fleet Quit After Fliers Bombed It; 300 Killed In Base Fight

Last Mutinous Ships Surrender In Chile, Ending Reds' Revolt

Employment Relief Plan Avoiding Income Tax Rise Offered By Republicans

Hoover And Roosevelt Differ Widely On Aid To The Idle In Red Cross Talks; Governor's Relief Plan Wins At Albany

Britain Imposes Big Tax Increases And Drastic Pay Cuts To End Deficit; Congress Leaders For New Levies Here

Hundreds Die In Hurricane At Belize; Tidal Wave Sweeps City; Porto Rico Hit; Third Gale Rushing On Western Mexico

1,000 Are Dead In Belize; Hurricane Ruins Burned; Town May Be Abandoned

Austria Puts Down A One-Day Revolt, Routing Heimwehr

Ocean Fliers Fight Wind On Way Here; Airports Keep Vigil Throughout Night; Plane Last Reported Nearing Halifax

Hoover Rejects Bank Plea To Extend His Moratorium; He Will Not Move For Beer

Body Of Collings Found, Limbs Tied; Mystery Deepens

Senate Republicans Defy Roosevelt, Pass Own Measure For State Relief; Governor Takes Fight To Public On Air

Japanese Seize Mukden In Battle With Chinese; Rush More Troops To City

Japanese Take All Towns On Manchuria Railroad; Defiance Of Tokyo Hinted

Great Britain Suspends Gold Payments Today; Closes Stock Exchange, Discount Rate Up To 6%, German Boerses Shut, Stock Market Here Open

Britain Calm Under Gold Suspension; Act Gets Royal Assent; Pound At $4.22; Stocks Rally Here After Early Slump

League Urges Peace On China And Japan; Seeks Our Support

Big Gamblers Operated In Chief Tammany Clubs, Police Captain Testifies

Murder In Tammany Club Unsolved Though Suspect Was Named To The Police

League Backs View On Japan And China; Drops Inquiry Plan

Famished Chinese Imperil Lindbergh; He Escapes In Plane

Sweden, Norway, Egypt Suspend Gold Standard; Others Likely To Follow

France And Germany Unite In Trade Cooperation Plan; To Develop Soviet Market

Episcopalians Vote For Liberal Divorce After Bitter Fight

OCTOBER

War Spirit In China Spreads To Capital; New Army To Train

$2,300,000,000 Deal Unites National City And Bank Of America

Lindberghs' Plane Capsizes In Yangtse

Pope Urges Aid For Idle, Laying Ills To Arms Race; Warns Of Peril To Society

Coll Seized With His Gang; Identified As Baby Killer; 6 Taken In Battle Upstate

Dwight W. Morrow Dies; Suffered Stroke In Sleep; World Leaders Mourn Him

Hoover Urges $500,000,000 Pool To Aid Banks, With Enlarged Federal Farm Loan System; Congress Leaders Agree To Support Program

Bankers Move To Speed Hoover's Plan, Widely Hailed As Constructive Effort; President Changed Phrases On Debts

Plans for Huge Credit Pool Complete; Further Moves Considered By Hoover, Including Federal Reserve Revision

Japan Reveals Aim To Hold Manchuria Until She Wins Friendly Regime There; Stimson To Act, League Council Called

Capone's Bodyguard At Trial Is Arrested

Hitler Unites Ranks Of The Old Germany To War On Bruening

China Threatens War As League Meets; Tokyo Warns Against Any Interference; Washington Backs Geneva In Grave Test

League Pledges All Efforts For Peace; Secret Session Today To Study Our Aid; Japanese Bomb 4 Chinese Troop Trains

League Ready To Invite US But Japan Delays Assent; Bandits Sweep Manchuria

League Council Votes 13-1 To Invite US Despite Strong Opposition Of Japan; Tokyo's Envoy Here Advises Yielding

American Sits With The League Council To Apply Kellogg Pact To Manchuria; Gets A Warm Welcome; Japan Objects

Capone Convicted Of Dodging Taxes; May Get 17 Years

World Mourns the Death Of Edison; Body to Lie in State in Laboratory

Japan Gives Her Consent To Our Sitting In League; Tension Much Lessened

$100,000,000 Rise In Rates Offered To Roads By I.C.C. If They Form Credit Pool

Lights of City Dimmed in Homage to Edison; The Nation Joins in the Brief Silent Tribute

Hoover Welcomes Laval At White House; Premier, Hailed Here, Pledges France To Peace And To Economic Cooperation

Hoover And Laval Confine Their Talks To Policies To Cut Short Depression; Borah Demands Peace Treaty Revision

League Sets Nov. 16 For Withdrawal Of The Japanese Troops In Manchuria; Russia Ready To Protect Her Interests

Hoover And Laval Agree On Steps To Bring World Economic Stability; Groundwork Laid For Debt Revision

Hoover Will Ask Congress To Cut Debts; Berlin Plans New Reparations Move; Laval Sails At Dawn After Seeing City

Conservative Landslide In Britain; National Cabinet's Return Assured; Labor Is Swamped, Liberals Crushed

Hoover Committee Offers A Program For Recovery; Gloomy Talk Is Deplored

Hoover Assails 'Untruths' By Navy League, Promising An Inquiry To Give Facts

Sherwood Assets Tied Up; Bus Line Official Has Key To Walker's Safety Box

NOVEMBER

Indian Constitution On American Model Emerges In London

Smith Plan Charged To Block Roosevelt; Governor To Retort

Japanese See Need For Further Attack To Clear Manchuria

Tammany Sweeps The City With Record Pluralities; Republicans Keep Assembly; Forestry Amendment Wins; House Will Be Democratic; Moore Victor In New Jersey

Expect League Call As Japanese Extend Sway In Manchuria

Japanese Defeat Chinese In Manchuria; League Council Called To Paris Nov. 17; Stimson Moves Again To Bring Peace

Chinese Flee Before Japanese Attack In 2-Day Battle At Manchurian Bridge; League Considering Diplomatic Break

Japanese Halt Pursuit, Fear Clash With Russia; Concern In Washington

Tientsin Is Shelled By Japanese Guns; Our Troops Stand By

New Clash In Manchuria; Washington To Act Again As Danger Of War Grows

Tokyo Repeats To Stimson Refusal To Recall Troops; New Shellfire In Tientsin

Resolution And Injunction Cannot Keep World Peace, Hoover Armistice Winning

Russians Strengthen Gen. Ma's Army, Sending Arms And Men To Fight Japan; Briand Makes New Appeal For Peace

Hoover Moves To Form Twelve Home Loan Banks As Spur To Construction

Ma Accepts Japan's Terms, Tokyo Hears; Hostile Action Ceases On Nonni River; Chinese Boy Emperor Reaches Mukden

Japanese Beat Back Big Chinese Force Attempting To Outflank Them On Nonni; League To Renew Peace Efforts Today

Grandi Calls On Hoover; Landing Here Is Avoided; Trip To Capital By Train

Grandi's Visit May Widen Geneva Arms Conference; Talks With Hoover Today

Japanese Capture Tsitsihar Station, And Press On To City After Battle; Tokyo Defies League; China Asks Help

Stimson Plans New Move With League To Win Tokyo To Moderation In China; Japanese Install Ally In Tsitsihar

Japan And China Reject The League Council Plan For A Truce And Inquiry

Emergency Cabinet Looms In Tokyo; Stimson Cautions Japanese On Russia; League Now Plans All-China Inquiry

League Draws Plan For Inquiry In China; Tokyo Parties Clash

New Battle Starts South Of Mukden; 'Real War' Is Seen

Japanese In Battle Twice Near Mukden; China Tells Terms

Warning By British Keeps Japanese From Chinchow; American To Join Inquiry

Heavy Fighting Is Raging In Tientsin; Japanese And Italians Shell Chinese After Attacks On Foreign Concessions

Big Japanese Force Moves On Chinchow Despite Shidehara's Pledge To Stimson; 18 Foreigners Killed In Tientsin Fight

Communists Behind The 'Hunger March' Moving On Capital

Chinese Offer A Truce In Manchuria; Chang To Move Troops From That Area; Japan Retracts Criticism Of Stimson

DECEMBER

Manchurian Accord Nearer As Chinese Drop Vital Demand

Walker In Dramatic Plea Asks Pardon For Mooney; Rolph To Speed Decision

Millikan Pictures Show Atom Smashed

Revolution In Salvador Ousts President Araujo; U.S. Envoy Ends Fighting

Hitler Backs Debts, Bars Reparations; Sees Victory Soon

Madison Av. Flooded, Hundreds Marooned, As A Main Bursts

Hitler Says Ballots Will Give Him Power; Scouts Talk Of Coup

Cheering Democrats Organize House Under Gardner As 72nd Congress Opens; Party Leaders Are Ready For Big Job

Hoover Message Calls For Tax Rise And $500,000,000 Credit Corporation; Fight Over Moses Deadlocks Senate

Mellon Asks Broad Rise In Income Tax, Also Levies On Autos, Radios, Checks; Democrats Voice Sharp Opposition

Hoover Wants War Debt Board Revived For 'Further Temporary Adjustments'; Strong Objection To Plan In Congress

Convicts Kidnap Warden; Escape At Leavenworth; 3 Die In Battle, 3 Caught

Minority Cabinet Is Formed In Japan; To Drop Gold Basis

Japan Quits Gold Basis; Nation Divided On Policy; New Clash In Manchuria

Hoover Says 'No Default' On Dec. 15 Debt Payments As Congress Debates Step

Tense Row In House On Moratorium; M'Fadden Charges Hoover 'Sold Out'; Mills Insists On Pledge To Ratify

Stimson Urges Speed On Moratorium; Points To Critical Conditions Abroad; Colleagues In House Assail M'Fadden

House Committee Reports Moratorium But Bars Debt Cuts Or Cancellation; London And Paris Act On Reparations

House Votes Moratorium By 317 To 100; Records Opposition To Debt Revision; Lamont Belittles Foreign Loan Peril

Mitchell Forecasts Debts Revision; Fears Reich, If Pressed, Will Revolt; Neutrals Seek End Of Reparations

J.W. Schatz Slain By Butler In Home; Women Guest Cut

Japanese In Manchuria To Stay, Observer Finds; Ruling Through Puppets

Senate Ratifies Moratorium, 69 to 12, After Johnson Attack On President; Traylor Scores Hoover Credit Pool

Experts Ask New Deal On Reparations; Assert Reich Cannot Resume Payments; Hoover Signs The Moratorium Measure

Reich Holds Young Plan 'Pulled Up By The Roots'; Borah Warns Washington

Paris And London Call Parley At Hague Jan. 18 On Reparations And War Debts; Washington Silent On Our Attitude

U.S. Will Get Invitation To Debt Parley At Hague; An Observer May Be Sent

Big Japanese Force Reaches Manchuria As New Drive Opens

Gandhi Warns India To Be Ready To Fight

Chang Gives Up Chinchow To Avert Attack On China; Japanese Are Pushing On

Mail Bomb Kills Two In Postoffice At Easton; Aimed At Fascists Here

1932: NEW YORK TIMES (366)

JANUARY

Six More Bombs Discoverd In 4 Cities; Point To Nation-Wide Anti-Fascist Plot; Government Spurs Hunt For Terrorists

Japan Takes Chinchow, Entering On Schedule After Chang Withdrawal

Cruisers To Become 'Little Battleships'; Navy Alters Design

Gandhi Sent To Jail; Party To Be Banned; All India Quits Work

Hoover Asks Speed On Relief Bills; Congress Chiefs Pledge Quick Action; Democrats Offer Their Tariff Plan

Raskob Urges Democrats To Unite On Wet Problem; Poll Is Heavily Anti-Dry

Roosevelt Calls For New Leadership In Nation, As He Cites State's Needs; Message Urges Emergency Tax Rise

Stimson Insists On Rights In Manchuria Under 9-Power Treaty And Kellogg Pact; Invites The Other Signatories To Act

Seabury Charges Culkin Embezzled Public Funds, Calls Hastings Paid Agent

Walker Asks Federal Aid, Denounces Bank 'Squeeze' On $90,000,000 Loan To City

Mob of 12,000 Frees 3 Prisoners in India; Wife of Gandhi is Placed Under Arrest

Senate Votes Reconstruction Bill, 63-8, But Rejects Walker Plea For City Aid; Mayor Orders Cut In Municipal Costs

Roosevelt Asks 100 Per Cent Increase In Tax On Incomes And Gasoline Sales To Meet Large Deficit Faced By State

European Problems Dropped By Hoover; 'Home Job' Put First

Nation's Democrats Rally For Victory; Roosevelt Calls For New Tax System; Hoover To Run, Spokesman Announces

Dr. Butler Assails 'Stupid Isolation' In Plea For League

'Militant Drive' Ordered To Obtain League Adherence

China Will Demand Sanctions By League Against Japanese

Japanese Planning A 'Free' Manchuria Dominated By Tokyo

City Gets $12,500,000 Loan For 11 Days At 6 Per Cent; Further Bank Aid Likely

Bankers Agree To Lend City $350,000,000 On Walker Pledge Of Strict Economy; Albany Quickly Passes Charter Relief

Germans Seek Truce At Home For A Year Without Elections

Hoover Reconstruction Plan In Effect; President Signs The $2,000,000,000 Bill; Dawes To Begin Operations Next Week

Gov. Roosevelt Enters Race For Presidency In North Dakota Primary

Seabury Finds City Needs New Rule With Non-Partisan Head To End Graft; Will Call Upon Legislature To Act

Crisis Near At Shanghai; Japanese May Block Port; Hoover Studies Situation

Shanghai Certain Japan Will Strike; Tension Increases

Washington Consults London On China; Tokyo's Ultimatum Ends At 5 A.M. Today; Martial Law In Shanghai Foreign Area

Japanese Unable To Occupy Shanghai Despite 13-Hour Land And Air Attack; Stimson Asks Tokyo To Tell Intention

Japanese Forced Back At Shanghai; Great Area In Ruins, Hundreds Slain; League Acts, U.S. And Britain Protest

Japanese Seize Part Of Foreign Area In Shanghai And Terrorize Residents; China Asks Aid, Makes Threat Of War

FEBRUARY

Our Asiatic Fleet, 1,600 Men, Sent To Shanghai; British Also Act; France And Italy Back Policy; Fighting Is Renewed In City; Battle Near Harbin

50,000 Chinese Troops Reach Shanghai; Japanese Shell Nanking And Land Men; Britain Joins U.S. In Vigorous New Note

Powers Unite In Peace Move For China, But Tokyo Objects To Some Proposals; Japanese Planes Again Bomb Shanghai

Washington Pledges 100 Per Cent Aid For Safety Of Shanghai Settlement; Tokyo Rejects Peace; Battle Goes On

Japanese Land Big Guns, Pound Chapei; Chinese Planes Engage Foe Near City; Tokyo Sends Infantry; Harbin Taken

Japanese Sailors Fail To Take Chapei; Tokyo Is Sending An Army Of 22,000; League Observers Report On Shanghai

Big Guns Reopen Battle At Shanghai; Chinese Mobilize 100 Fighting Planes; Japanese Troops Land At Woosung

Japanese Advance On Woosung Forts As Navy Makes New Attack At Chapei; Tokyo Asks Foreign Rule In 5 Cities

Japanese Mass On Chapei; Checked Around Woosung; U.S. Upholds 9-Power Pact

Chinese Hold Off Enemy On Three Lines Of Attack; Inouye Is
Slain In Tokyo

Action To Aid Bank Credits And Free Billions In Gold Agreed On
At White House

Congress Gets Credit Expansion Bill; Hailed As Marking End Of
Deflation; Stock Prices Up $3,000,000,000 Here

Fighting In Shanghai Threatens To Widen; Firing Worst Yet

2,000 Killed And Wounded In Fierce Woosung Fight; Japanese
Land 10,000 Men

Chinese Mass Big Army At Shanghai As More Japanese Troops Are
Landed; League Envoys Report 'State Of War'

Shanghai Expects Battle On Two Fronts Tomorrow; Powers Try To
Prevent It

Tokyo Says Stimson Plans Stern Note; Warning By League Invokes
Article X; Japanese Shell Foe, Issue Ultimatum

Chinese Join Peace Move;, But Say They Won't Yield Unless
Japanese Retreat

China Will Reject Japanese Demands; Troops, Planes, Guns Ready
For Battle; Manchuria Proclaims Separate State

Japanese Open Shanghai Offensive; Each Army Claims The
Advantage After A Day Of Stubborn Fighting

Chinese Cling To Lines Under Terrific Attack; Kiangwan Village
Changes Hands Three Times; Japanese Troops Press Assault Behind
Tanks

Japanese Push 2 Miles Past Kiangwan, But The Chinese Hold Fast To Village; Vote In Japan Backs Military Party

Chinese Drive Foe Back At Shanghai; Their Guns Set Fires In Foreign Area; Japan To Rush Troop Reinforcements

Japan Speeds New Army To Shanghai; Chinese Drive Enemy Back Two Miles; Tokyo Stands Firm In Reply To League

Stimson Holds Pacific Treaty Broken; Sees Tokyo Voiding Naval Pact Ratio; Japanese Again Try To Take Kiangwan

Chinese Claim Victory In Night Battle After Hardest Open Fight At Shanghai; Tokyo Contradicts Stimson On Treaties

Chinese Drive Enemy Out Of Mioshin, Blocking Move To Bottle Up Kiangwan; Japanese, In Raid, Down Three Planes

Japan Lands Fresh Troops At Shanghai; Again Offers Truce If Chinese Retreat; Kiangwan Holds Out As Foe Makes Gain

Peace Negotiations Begun At Shanghai; Prospects Of Accord 'Fair,' Tokyo Says; Fighting Goes On, New Drive On Chapei

MARCH

Demands Of Japanese And Chinese Balk Peace Moves At Geneva
And Shanghai; New Drive Is Opened Against Chinese

Lindbergh Baby Kidnapped From Home Of Parents On Farm Near
Princeton; Taken From His Crib; Wide Search On

Lindbergh Hopeful, Is Ready To Ransom Son; Nation's Greatest
Hunt For Kidnappers Pushed; All Clues Thus Far Futile; Country
Is Shocked

No Trace Of Lindbergh Kidnappers; 300 Questioned, Servants
Exonerated; Parents By Radio Ask Return Of Boy

Friend Of Lindbergh Nurse Is Seized At Hartford Where Card Was
Mailed; No Reply To Parents' Appeal For Son

Lindberghs In Message To Abductors Name Two Men To Represent
Them In Negotiations For Return Of Baby

Lindberghs Fail To Reach Kidnappers Through Underworld
Go-Betweens; Sailor Held In Jersey, Chum Questioned

Two Notes Received From Kidnappers; Police To Let Col.
Lindbergh Negotiate Directly For Return Of Stolen Child

Progress Made In Search For The Lindbergh Baby; Lawyer On
Secret Mission

Lindbergh Search Pressed Near Home; Moore Is Confident

Hindenburg Appeals For Votes To Avert Victory Of Radicals

Police Issue Appeal To Nation In Search For Lindbergh Baby

German Election In Doubt On Eve Of The Vote Today; Discontent Aids Radicals

Hindenburg Barely Fails Of Election; Polls 7,333,165 More Votes Than Hitler; Considered Certain To Win In Run-Off

Eastman A Suicide; Note To His Friends Says 'Work Is Done'

Japan Agrees To Go From Shanghai Area

Builder Denounces Flynn For Persecution And Ruin; Bronx Official On Stand

Hitler Centres Raided on Civil War Rumor; He Admits Order to 500,000 to Fight Reds

Coalition Routs Leaders On Tax Bill, Forcing War-Time Surtax On Wealth; Vote 153 To 87; Sales Levy In Peril

Legal 4% Beer Proposed By Senate Subcommittee As An Economic Measure

Tokyo's War Office Halts Peace Plans; Armies Near Clash

Shanghai Foes Sign Truce Agreement

De Valera Notifies Britain Irish Will End Royal Oath; Conflict May Go To Court

Britain Warns Irish Oath Is Mandatory; Negotiation Hinted

House Kills The Sales Tax, 223 To 153; 'Nuisance' Levies Now To Be Proposed; Coalition Refuses To Take Leadership

Hoover Demands Budget Be Balanced As Keystone Of Business Recovery; Beer Tax Beaten; Oil 'Tariff' Is Voted

New Coalition Votes Tariff On Coal; Pleas By Crisp And Other Leaders Halt Drive To Put More Duties In Tax Bill

Seabury For Reform Of Lower Courts To Rid Them Of Politics And Graft, Ending Mayor's Right To Name Judges

Flies to Lindbergh To Report Contact With Kidnappers

Garner Gets Pledge To Balance Budget; House Votes $158,500,000 Sales Taxes; President Warns He Will Veto Bonus

Governor Backs M'Quade, Denouncing Ouster Move; Walker 'Ready To Testify'

APRIL

Angry Democrats Block Seabury On Hastings Writ; Flynn Talks, Avoids Jail

House Completes $1,032,400,000 Tax Bill; Surtax Rates Cut; Dividend Levy Voted; Treasury Holds Budget Not Balanced

4-Year Federal War On Chicago Gangs Told By Prosecutor

Hoover Expected To Ask A $300,000,000 Budget Cut; Tax Bill's Foes Mobilize

Mrs. Fosdick Kills 2 Children And Self

Hoover Outlines Economy Program; Demands Congress Set Up Joint Board; Legion Head Backs President On Bonus

Curtis Says He Met Kidnappers' Agent; Told Baby Was Well

Offer Of 'Favors' For Willard Data A Joke, Flynn Says

Stimson Is Hopeful Of New Curb On War; Sails For Geneva

Lindbergh Paid A Ransom Of $50,000, But Kidnappers Did Not Return Child, He Announces After Waiting For Days

Hindenburg Wins Election; Hitler Is 6,000,000 Behind; Communists Lose Heavily

Liquidation, Not Shorts, Upset Stocks, Says Whitney; Promises List Of Bears; 11% Salary Cut Is Pushed In House

Condon Deals Anew With Kidnappers And Reassures Them

Smith's Call For New War Debt Deal And Veiled Challenge To Roosevelt Stir Democrats At Jefferson Fete

Massie Tells Jury Of Attack On Wife; Insanity Is Defense

Tammany Controls State Delegation; Smith And Davis On It; Wet Plank Voted; Walker Plans Big Beer Parade May 14

Massie Takes Blame In Hawaiian Murder; Can't Recall Firing

Soviet Army Force Doubled In Far East; Japanese Disturbed

Whitney Says Short Sales Saved Market Last Fall; Bears' Names Kept Secret

British Budget Omits Debt Payments; Does Not Provide $171,500,000 Due To US; Official Washington Is Not Surprised

Senate's Sharp Economies Worry Hoover And Mills; Loss Of 6,000 Jobs Is Seen

Tokyo War Minister Defies The League

Inquiry Denounced In Ruling By Court As Defaming City

Experts Say Massie Did Not Lose Sanity

Nazis Lead In Four States; Win 162 Seats In Prussia; Liberals Now In Minority

Japan Strengthens Manchurian Army

Smith Sweep In Bay State; His Race With Roosevelt In
Pennsylvania Is Close

Hoover Asks Nation-Wide Tax Reform; Calls On Governors To
Help Recovery; Senate Bill Doubles Income Tax Rate

Bomb At Shanghai Wounds 5 High Japanese Officials; Shirakawa
And Uyeda Hit

Manslaughter Is Verdict For Four In Massie Trial; Jury Asks For
Leniency

MAY

Honolulu Divided By Massie Verdict; Patrol Guard City

Atom Torn Apart, Yielding 60% More Energy Than Used

Capone Plea Denied By Supreme Court

House Votes Economy Bill With Only $38,124,000 Left Of Its $206,000,000 Saving

All In Massie Case Freed After Serving One Hour; Will Drop Assault Charge

Hoover Sends Congress Sharp Message, Saying Its Inaction Disturbs The Nation; Demands Quick Balancing Of Budget

French President Dies Of His Wounds 14 Hours After Being Shot By Russian; Two Others Wounded Defending Him

French Seek Unity As Nation Mourns; Slayer Called A Red

Left Triumphs In France; Tardieu Coalition Beaten; Herriot Likely Successor

Young To Be Put Up As A 'Dark Horse' If Roosevelt Fails

Hastings In Rage Menaces Seabury, Causing Uproar; 'Blackmailer,' He Shouts

$2,300,000,000 Relief Proposed To Senate In Democratic Plan

Lindbergh Baby Found Dead Near Home; Murdered Soon After The Kidnapping 72 Days Ago And Left Lying In Woods

Hunt For Slayers Of Lindbergh Baby Centres On Gangsters Who Got Ransom; President Orders Relentless Search

Condon Knows Man He Paid $50,000 In Lindbergh Case; Planes Hunt Gang At Sea

Militarists Kill The Premier In Tokyo, Bomb Banks, Police In A Day Of Terror; Seventeen In Uniform Then Surrender

Lindley Expedition Scales Mt. M'Kinley; Descending, Finds Carpe And Koven Dead; Young Scientists Fell Into A Crevasse

Curtis Admits He Hoaxed Lindbergh In Kidnap Hunt; Grew 'Insane On Subject'

Curtis Is Jailed For Hoax; Peacock Asked Lindbergh To Post $25,000, Police Say

12 Bankers And Industrialists To Find Ways To Use Federal Reserve Credit; Hoover Approves New Recovery Move

Walker Used $10,000 Letter Of Credit Bought By Bus Man For Trip To Europe; Got It Day Before Signing Franchise

Financier Of Walker Trip Forced Back From Europe; Mayor Defies His Accuser

Roosevelt Demands 'National Income' Be Redistributed

Walker's Income Tax Under Inquiry; Sherwood Collected Fees For Mayor, Got $51,960 For Stocks Worth $29,000

Europe Will Pay US Delayed Annuities Over 10-Year Period

Mayor On Stand Angrily Defends Acts And Accuses Seabury Of
Persecution; Admits Gift Of $246,692 Stock Profit

Walker, Concluding, Derides Charges; Denies Link With
Sherwood's $700,000; Rebukes The Inquiry As Destructive

Hoover Condemns 'Pork Barrel' Relief; Calls On People To Halt
Garner Plan; Senate Votes $270,000,000 New Taxes

Sales Tax Quarrel Grips The Senate; Hoover Criticized

Seabury Is Ready To Draft Charges Against Walker

Tax Agreement Is Reported Reached At Parley Of Hoover And
Democrats;, Balancing Budget Without Sales Levy

JUNE

Senate Passes $1,115,000,000 Tax Bill; Balances Budget After
Hoover Plea; $238,000,000 Economy Measure Reported

Dr. Walker Admits Doctors For City Split Fees With Him; Banked
$431,258; Mayor Proved Unfit, Seabury Declares

Action To Remove Walker Is Left To Gov. Roosevelt; Seabury
Delays Charges

Roosevelt To Get Walker Case At Once; Seabury Accepts Challenge
To Act As Governor Scores 'Political Sniping'

Socialist Revolt In Chile Upsets Montero Regime; Davila In The
New Junta

Hoover And Finance Board Propose Loans For Jobless And New
Aid For Farmers

John D. Rockefeller Jr. Out For Repeal; Says Dry Law Evils
Outweigh Benefits; Urges Wet Planks In Both Platforms

Leaders Of 2,500,000 Wets Unite To Fight For Repeal; Spurred By
Rockefeller

Seabury Puts Walker Data In The Hands Of Roosevelt; Gives No
Opinion On Course

League Body Asks World To Go Back To Gold Standard

Morrow Maid Ends Life; Suspected In Kidnapping; Friend With Record Seized

Prohibition Battle Lines Are Drawn By Republicans Gathering At Chicago; Fight Over The Vice Presidency Looms

Republican Repealists Begin Drive; New York's Delegation Takes Lead; Hoover Aides Striving For Control

Hoover Men Draft Mild Wet Plank; Repeal Fight On Floor Held Certain; President Likely To Speak For Curtis

Hoover Approves Dry-Wet Prohibition Plank; His Steam Roller Crushes Threatened Revolt; Convention Receives Keynote Speech Coolly

Convention Adopts Hoover Dry-Wet Plank; Repealists Wage A Futile Battle On Floor; Uproar Among Delegates And In Galleries

Hoover, Curtis Renamed On First Ballots; Dry-Wet Plank Is Defended By Stimson

President Takes Up Plans For Campaign With Aides; Economic Issue Put First

France Sees Europe United Against US On War-Debt Issue

Vannie Higgins Dies, Silent On Slayers; Police Mystified

Borah Bolts Hoover On The Wet Plank; Holds Republicans Pledged To Repeal; Intends To Carry Issue 'To The People'

Herriot Rejects Our Plan For Reductions Of Armies; Bars Ending Reparations

Hoover Asks Arms Cuts Of One-Third To Save More Than $10,000,000,000; Italy Accepts, Others To Ask Changes

Drive To Abolish The Two-Thirds Rule Agreed Upon By Roosevelt Delegates; Smith Admits Governor Has 570 Votes

Roosevelt Forces Spurn Compromise; Stake All On Ending Two-Thirds Rule; Smith And Glass Lead Fight To Keep It

Lewis Quits Race, Frees Delegates; Roosevelt Gets 28 Of Illinois Votes; Plank For Submission Of Repeal Ready

Roosevelt Has A Lead On Rule Change Despite Loss Of 65 New York Votes; Platform Draft Links Debts And Arms

Roosevelt Orders Two-Thirds Rule Fight End, But Backers In Committee Take Issue To Floor; Delegates Wildly Cheer Barkley's Repeal Plea

Roosevelt's Forces Seat Walsh, 626 To 528; Forced To Yield In Two-Thirds Rule Fight; Revolt By Ultra-Wets Holds Up Platform

Democrats Pledge Party To Repeal Of The Dry Law And Quick Modification To Legalize Beer, 934 3/4-213 3/4; Plank Against War Debt Cancellation Is Submitted

JULY

First Ballot: Roosevelt 666 1/4; Smith 201 3/4; Tammany Poll On Floor Delays The Vote

Roosevelt Nominated On Fourth Ballot; Garner Expected To Be His Running Mate; Governor Will Fly To Convention Today

Roosevelt Puts Economic Recovery First In His Acceptance Speech At Convention; Garner For Vice President By Acclamation

Roosevelt Plans Aggressive Campaign, Carrying Fight To 'Republican' States; Wet Victory In South Spurs Beer Drive

Italy Urges Europe To Cancel War Debt And End Reparation

Hoover Halts Relief Bill; Holds A Night Conference To Have Measure Changed

Hoover-Garner Tilt Halts Relief Bill; President Opposes A Broad Loan Basis; Speaker Charges 'Class Legislation'

British Ask Cut Of Third In Size Of Ships And Guns; Would Limit Air Bombing

Lausanne Accord Ends Reparations; Berlin To Issue $714,000,000 In Bonds; Washington Open To Debt Overtures

Hoover Would Consider Capacity To Pay But Still Opposes Canceling War Debts; Pact Signed, Ratification Waits On US

Ibanez Vainly Tries Army Coup In Chile; Is Again A Refugee

Commons Told We Joined In Lausanne Debt Talks; Reich Disowns Secret Pact

No Debt Pledge Given By Washington, No Secrecy, M'Donald Tells Commons; Stimson Insists That We Kept Aloof

$5,000,000 Blaze Sweeps Coney Island; Four Blocks On Boardwalk Destroyed; Huge Crowds Watch Six-Hour Battle

Hoover Warns Europe On United Front On Debts, Denying We Were Consulted; Britain Insists Pact Will Not Affect US

Deadlock Over The Relief Bill Broken; Congress Expected To Adjourn Today; Hoover Cuts Pay $15,000, Cabinet 15%

72D Congress Adjourns Near Midnight; Relief And Home Loan Bank Bills Pass; Senate In Flurry Over Dry Law Repeal

10,000 Die In Battles In 5 Areas Of China

13 Policemen Suspended As Nassau Inquiry Bares Third Degree Brutality

Prussian Dictator Demanded By Nazis

Reich Seizes Prussia, Names Dictator; Army Ousts Officials And Rules Berlin; Papen Acts Under Hindenburg's Orders

I.C.C. Approves 4 Eastern Rails Systems; New England Consolidation Deferred; Wabash-Seaboard Project Is Canceled

Walker Calls On 147,000 City Employes To Give Up Month's Pay, Saving $26,000,000; Warns Albany Will Act If They Don't

Employes Of City Accepting Pay Cut As Necessity Now

Italy Now Building Warships In Secret, Says British Expert

Court Backs Papen On Dictatorship; He Will Curb Army

Reich Ready to Arm in Defiance of Treaty, Says Schlicher, if Others Don't Disarm

Warn City To Slash Budget, Cut Realty By $3,000,000,000

Troops Drive Veterans From Capital; Fire Camps There And At Anacostia; 1 Killed, Scores Hurt In Day Of Strife

Bonus Stragglers 'Mopped Up' By Troops; 36 Reds Seized; Grand Jury Inquiry On; Hoover Denounces Attempt At Mob Rule

Bonus Army At Johnstown Stirs Protest By Citizens; State Guard Is Refused

AUGUST

Right Parties Fail To Carry Germany; Nazi Seats Doubled

7 Firemen Killed, 31 Injured By Blast In Ritz Tower Hotel

Reich Would Seek Private Debts Cut At World Parley

B.E.F. Begins Disbanding; Going To Homes By Train; Hurley Defends Hoover

Firemen Reject Pay Cut By A Vote Of 4,900 To 278; Block Walker Economy

Carr Of U.S. Wins Title At Olympics; Sets World Record

Cotton Mills Organizing To Buy Out Farm Board; Stocks Rise 2 To 12 Points

State Asked To Void Dr. Walker's License For Splitting Fees

Walker Insists On Right To Cross-Examine Seabury At The Roosevelt Hearing

Reich Will Enforce Curb On Riots Today; Nazi Coup Rumored

Hitler Is Expected To Be Chancellor In Cabinet Shake-Up

Governor Queries Mayor On Sisto Bonds; Curbs Oratory But Allows Witnesses; Walker Pleads For His Official Life

Mayor Denies Block's $246,000 Was Gift; Contradicts Hastings's Bus Testimony; Writ Suit Aug. 19; Won't Halt Roosevelt

Hitler Demands Office As Dictator; Hindenburg Bars It

15 Injured As Bomb Explodes In Movie

Walker Must Explain Sherwood Deals, Governor Refusing To Drop Charges; Mayor Wants To Subpoena 12 Witnesses

'Wish Sherwood Were Here,' Cries Mayor, As Governor Presses His Questioning; 'Unnamed Person' Revealed As Woman

Walker Defends Brother On Split Fees; Mayor Will Summon 12 Witnesses Today; Curtin, Rebuked, Calls Governor Biased

Mayor Gets Writ To Bar Removal Action; Governor's Powers To Be Argued Today; Defense Subpoenas Republican Chiefs

Mollison Flies Atlantic To St. John, N.B., Keeping Course Despite Winds And Fog; Visits Montreal Today; New York Later

Roosevelt Demands Federal Control Of Stock And Commodity Exchanges; Denounces Hoover Economic Policies

Roosevelt Ponders Appeal For Funds To 'Forgotten Man'

Witnesses Defend Mayor On Taxi Law, Denying Favoritism Or Monopoly Plan; Won't Block Governor, Court Indicates

Block And Ungerleider Deny Asking Or Getting Favors From The Mayor; Roosevelt Amazed By Sherwood Deal

Governor Bars Republicans From Stand, Holds Testimony On 'Plot' Irrelevant; Delaney Testifies At First Night Session

Governor And Hilly Clash On Ethics Of Split Fees; Walker Backed
On Buses

Hoover Sees Major Crisis Overcome; Conference Adopts Revival
Program; Bank Foreclosures On Homes Halted

Revival Program Begun With Move To Spread Jobs; A.F. Of L.
Backs The Drive

'Ma' Ferguson Ahead In Close Texas Race

Court Refuses To Halt Walker Hearing, Upholds Governor's Power
Of Removal, But Calls Procedure At Trial Unfair

Clouds Threaten To Mar The Eclipse In Wide Area Today

SEPTEMBER

Millions Here Watch Solar Eclipse; Clouds Mar Spectacle For
Science At Many Points In Totality Belt

Walker Resigns, Denouncing The Governor; Says He Will Run For
The Mayoralty Again, Appealing To 'Fair Judgment' Of The People

Fusion Ticket Against Walker Likely; Tammany Opens Fight On
Governor; M'Kee Takes Office, Pledges Economy

Walker Likely Not To Run, As Leaders Seek To Avoid Open Break
With Governor

100,000 In Military Review Cheered By Berlin Throng; World War
Chiefs Hailed

Paul Bern A Suicide; Wed Jean Harlow

M'Kee Slashes Own And Aides' Pay, Breaks Up City Printing
Monopoly; M'Cooey Will Work For Roosevelt

M'Kee Is Boomed To Oppose Walker If Latter Runs In Election On
Nov. 8; Mayor To Force Cuts In Fixed Salaries

Raymond Robins Vanishes On His Way To Visit Hoover;
Threatened By Liquor Ring

37 Dead, 64 Hurt In Explosion On Boat Crowded With Rikers
Island Workers; 8 Missing, Many Saved In East River

Walker Sails For Italy On Health Trip Of 20 Days; Doubt On
Candidacy Grows

Hutchinsons Feared Lost; Plane With 8 Down At Sea; Aid Goes
From Greenland

M'Kee Discharges Dwyer For Bronx Market Failure; Sues To Bar
Fall Election

Hoover Asks New And Stronger Effort, Laying Maine Upset To
The Depression; Democrats And Wets Hail Their Victory

Roosevelt Maps Farm Relief Program, Pledges Tariff Aid In Topeka
Speech; Hoover Policies Declared A Failure

Hoover Calls On Nation To Let No One Go Hungry Or Cold In
Coming Winter

Papen Overcoming Hostility Of States To Reform Of Reich

Roosevelt Outlines 6-Point Rail Plan; Would End Competition,
Control Buses, Protect Owners And 1,700,000 Workers

Britain Condemns German Arms Plea; Backs French View

3,000 Besiege Police After Boy Is Slain In Jersey Labor Riot

Hoover Wants The Reich To Remain In Arms Parley; Aloof On
Equality Plea

Regulation By Government Of Utilities And Federal Ownership Of
Power Sites Urged By Roosevelt To Protect Public

France Supports US On Manchuria Issue; Japan Scents A Deal

Roosevelt Renews Demand For Repeal; Praises Smith Amid Cheers Of 16,000; Tammany Decides To Fight For Governor

Hindus Sign Accord; Gandhi Gives Assent

M'Donald Approves Pact Among Hindus To End Gandhi's Fast

De Valera Declares League Is On Trial As Assembly Opens

Hurricane Kills 200 In Puerto Rico, Hurts 1,000, Causes Huge Property Loss; Virgin Islands, Dominican Republic Hit

Germany Puts Off Debt Payment To US

Tammany, In A Deal, Flouts Roosevelt, Names Hofstadter For Supreme Court; Election Of Mayor Nov. 8 Is Ordered

OCTOBER

Berry Strips M'Kee Of Budget Powers; Roosevelt Asks M'Cooey To Aid Lehman; Curry Seeks Deal With Walker Threat

M'Kee Now Ready To Run As Independent; To Carry Budget Row To People By Radio; Roosevelt Will Make Fight For Lehman

League Experts Find Japan At Fault, With Treaties Violated, In Manchuria; Can't Undo What's Done, Tokyo Retorts

Lehman's Nomination Appears Certain As Roosevelt And Smith Warn Curry; Republicans To Name Donovan Today

Col. Lehman Nominated For Governor; Curry Routed As His Allies Desert Him; Smith And Gov. Roosevelt Shake Hands

M'Kee Holds City Convention Illegal; Bronx To Bolt If One Is Held Tonight; Smith Leads Fight To Block Walker

Surrogate O'Brien Is Nominated For Mayor As Walker Withdraws; Leaders Ignore M'Kee; Court Of Appeals Orders Election On Nov. 8

O'Brien Pledges Economy, 5-Cent Fare; Pay Cuts Unlikely; M'Kee Won't Run; Republicans Press Hunt For Candidate

Republicans Name L.H. Pounds For Mayor; Candidate Pledges Fight For Economy; Bench Deal Won't Block 'Tin Box' Issue

Rebels Now Control Most Of Manchuria

Einstein Will Head School Here, Opening Scholastic Centre

Coolidge Says The Nation Needs Hoover; Recovering Starting, He Tells Rally Here; He Assails Roosevelt Silence On Bonus

Canada And Britain Adjust Tariff In Favor Of Empire; Our Exports Will Be Cut

Roosevelt Holds Relief An Obligation Of Nation; For 'Sound' Public Works

Reich Bars Geneva For 4-Power Talks On Equality Demand

Banks Bar City Loan Pending Economies; Hold Walker Promises Were Not Kept; Berry Rebuffed, Nov. 1 Pay Is In Peril

Hoover Appeals To Nation For 'Neighborhood' Relief; Baker Sees 'Call To Duty'

Banks Force $75,000,000 City Budget Cut; 50-Year Subway Financing Is Adopted; 5-Cent Fare Sacrificed, M'Kee Asserts

Roosevelt Calls Donovan Utility Ally In Two Speeches For The State Ticket; Lehman, Here, Pledges Liberal Rule

Roosevelt Opposes Cash Bonus Now; Urges Beer Tax To Balance Budget; Smith Pledges Loyalty In Speech Here

Threats To Voters' Jobs Are Charged By Roosevelt As Indianapolis Hails Him

Profound Changes Forecast In China

Hoover Denounces Roosevelt Program; Scores Democrats As
Trouble Makers; Lists Ten Signs Of Economic Recovery

Mussolini Appeals To US To Cut Debts; Will Stay In League

Smith Assails Hoover's 'Broken Pledges' As Newark Throng Cheers
Him Wildly; Governor, In Atlanta, Talks Of Markets

Roosevelt Likens The Administration To Four Horsemen

Japan Tries To Get Franco-Soviet Help In Manchurian Issue

Smith Appeals For Roosevelt In Boston; Hoover Off To Indiana On
Fighting Trip

Hoover In Direct Attack On Roosevelt Charges 'New Deal' Is Now
A 'Shuffle'; Scores Remark On The Supreme Court

London Fears Riots Of Jobless Today

Banks Lend City $18,500,000 But Demand Real Economy And A
Cut In All Salaries

NOVEMBER

Roosevelt, In Boston, Urges 5-Day Week, Federal Aid For Idle, Saying Hoover Failed To Use Own Economic Program

London Police Repel Raid By Jobless On Parliament In Three Hours Of Rioting

Jobless In Retreat, Mission A Failure; London Is Relieved

Roosevelt Denounces Hoover's Tactics; Charge Rule 'By Guess And By Gamble'; Young Condemns Republicans' 'Threats'

Hoover Sees Wets Misled By Promises Of Democrats; Defends Dawes Bank Loan

Hoover And Roosevelt End Campaigns, Governor At Big Tammany Rally Here, President With A Speech At St. Paul

Hitler's Vote Cut, Communists Gain, In Reich Election

Hoover And Roosevelt Make Final Pleas, With Nation Going To The Polls Today; Leaders Of Both Parties Claim Victory

Roosevelt Winner In Landslide! Democrats Control Wet Congress; Lehman Governor, O'Brien Mayor

Roosevelt Pledges Recovery Fight; Latest Count Assures Him 42 States; Quick Action On Liquor Is Expected

1,000 Are Dead In Hurricane In Cuba; Town Wiped Out, Cane Fields Ruined; Heavy Damage Caused Here By Gale

Roosevelt Is In Bed With A Slight Cold; 3-Day Rest Planned

Churchmen Favor Anti-War Embargo

Hoover Invites Roosevelt To Confer With Him On War Debts, Armaments And Economic Parley; London And Paris Debt Revision Notes Given Out

Roosevelt Agrees To Informal Talk, Puts Debt Responsibility On Hoover; Congress Action By Dec. 15 Doubtful

Row Over 50-Year Bonds Imperils The New Subway And City Budget Savings

President Will Not Request Congress To Suspend War Debt Payments Dec. 15; Further Study Depends On Roosevelt

M'Kee Gets Strong Backing; Tammany Chiefs, Alarmed By Crusade, Plan Savings

Dry Agents Find Robins In North Carolina Hills; Called Amnesia Victim

Hoover Plans $700,000,000 Cut In Costs To Balance Budget Without New Taxes; Will Seek The Cooperation Of Congress

Japan Relies To Lytton On Eve Of League Debate; Makes Self-Defense Plea

Hoover For Debt Delay And Settlement Review If Roosevelt Will Agree

Hoover Will Oppose Debt Suspension But Make Move For Possible
Revision; Roosevelt Non-Committal In Parley

Roosevelt Opposes Debt Commission As Proposed In Statement By
Hoover, But Would Hear Debtors Separately

France Will Offer Political Reasons In Another Request For Debt
Revision; Washington Awaits New British Rule

House Vote On Dry Repeal Agreed To By Both Parties; First
Business Of Session

Britain Prepares 'Human' Debt Appeal To Win Our Public Opinion
To Delay; Business Here Opposes Cancellation

Cold Kills 2 Here; Lodging Houses Full With Mercury At 12

Persia Cancels Vast British Oil Concession; Teheran Rejoices,
London Will Fight Decree

City Balked In Financing Its December Relief Fund; New
Economies Demanded

DECEMBER

City Asks Governor For Special Session In Move To Slash Salaries $20,000,000; Bankers See Real Economy Under Way

Britain Warns Dec. 15 Payment Imperils Lausanne, Recovery And Trade With US; Plea Moves Hoover But Not Congress

France Holds President Obligated To Debt Delay As Sequel To Moratorium

Democrats Expect Soviet Recognition

'Lame Duck' Congress Assembles Today To Act On Debts, Taxes, Beer, Farm Aid; House To Take Up Repeal As Gavel Falls

Dry Repeal Loses In House Vote, Vote 272-144, Wets Short 6 As 81 Lame Ducks Say Nay; Extra Session Of New Congress Likely

Hoover Message Calls For Sales Tax, Pay Cuts, Economy And Bank Reform; House Is Working On 2.75% Beer Bill

$40,000,000 Loan Averts Default By City; New Budget Cut Of $20,000,000 Pledged; Bankers Dictate Step, Curry Backs It

Hoover Offers Britain Review Of Debts In A New Note, But Bars Cancellation; Will Accept 'Any Appropriate Agency'

Roosevelt Asks Sweeping City Reforms And State Control Of Defaulting Towns In Calling On Legislature For Pay Cuts

Japan Seeks A Rise In Her Naval Ratio And Tonnage Slash

British Offer Payment In Gold On Dec. 15 On Condition It Apply
In New Deal On Debts; Stimson Promptly Rejects Terms As Illegal

Herriot Lays Debt Snarl To Hoover; Says France Will Pay With
Conditions; Britain To Meet Stimson's Objections

Herriot Falls, Deputies Vote Default, Refusing Payment Without
New Deal; Britain Will Pay, Belgium Will Not

Hoover For Debt Review With Britain; Will Ask Congress To Join
Discussion; Confusion In France; Poland Defaults

Hoover Plans To Seek Roosevelt's Aid In Arranging Debt Parley
With Britain; London Pays; Paris Still Seeks Cabinet

M'Kee On City Tour Hails Relief Work*

Senate Votes Bill To Free Philippines At End Of 12 Years

20,000 Jobless Get Work Clearing Snow From City's Streets

Hoover Asks Congress For Debt Board; He Wants Roosevelt To
Help Name It; Governor, Silent, Expected To Refuse

Roosevlet Bars Bipartisan Debt Action; Declines To Cooperate In
Naming Board, But Won't Hamper Immediate Review

House Authorizes 3.2% Beer, 230 To 165; All Of Drys'
Amendments Defeated; Senate Gets Bill Today, Fate In Doubt

Hoover Leaves War Debts To Roosevelt; He Suggested Naming
Young Or House; Governor Denies Refusing Cooperation

Beer By Christmas Defeated As Senate Demands More Time

Boy Is Lost In Creek; 12 Rescuers Hurt

Chinese In Jehol Battle Japanese; New Invasion Seen

Million Soviet Reds Face Party Ouster To Cut Inefficiency

Seabury Offers Draft Of City Charter To Oust Tammany And To
Unify Boards; Final Report Assails Budget Waste

'Prince Mike' Seized Near Fifth Av. Shop; Trapped by His Taste for
Costly Tobacco

O'Brien Plan Merges City Bureaus, Rejects Any Basic Charter
Change; $18,000,000 Pay Cuts Voted For Jan. 15

Mussolini Will Curb Industrial Output As a Means of Combating
Depression

1933: NEW YORK TIMES (365)

JANUARY

Nation's Scientists Honor Eyring At 32 For Atomic Studies

Long-Range Social Plan For Nation Urged By Hoover Board To Stabilize Economic System And Curb Unrest

State Needs Federal Aid For Jobless, Says Lehman In His Inaugural Speech; Roosevelt For New Nation-States Tie

Hoover, Back, Denounces Democrats For Blocking His Reorganization Plan

Lehman Urges Beer Law, Relief, Labor Legislation; Wins Republicans' Praise

Coolidge Dies Suddenly In His Northampton Home; The Former President, 60, Victim Of Heart Attack; Nation Is In Mourning; Hoover Will Attend Funeral

Coolidge Will Be Laid To Rest Today After Simple Northampton Services; Cabinet Joins Hoover For Funeral

Coolidge Buried With His Ancestors On Rain-Drenched Vermont Hillside; Hoover and Nation Pay Last Tribute

Princeton To Play Harvard In 1934; End Football Rift

Income Tax Rise Shelved; Democrats Now Counting On Drastic Economies

Japan Opens Jehol Drive; Fights Chinese For Pass; 3 Armies Ready To Move

4 Japanese Armies Advance In Jehol In Sub-Zero Gales

Hoover Gave Laval No Debt Pledge; He Insisted Congress Opposed Cuts; French Ability To Pay Was Stressed

Wine Added To Beer Bill; Alcohol Is Cut To 3.05% In Redraft For Senate

Japan Sees League Giving Way On Issue Of Free Manchukuo

Filibusters By Senators Block Vital Legislation; Party Leaders Worried

Stimson Reasserts Manchuria Policy As League Moves To Take Firm Stand; Assured Roosevelt Won't Alter It

Philippines Independence Plan Voted, Senate Overriding Hoover Veto, 66-26; Manila Hostile, Forecasts Rejection

Roosevelt To Meet Hoover Tomorrow For Survey Of The Foreign Situation; Extra Session Sure As Program Fails

Roosevelt And Stimson Talk Policies On Eve Of White House Conference; Speed On War Debts Comes To Fore

Roosevelt, Through Hoover, Invites Britain To Talk Debts After March 4; Way Paved For Other Powers In Turn

Government Operation Of Muscle Shoals Plant Pledged By Roosevelt

Palaces Of XerXes And Darius Dug Up In Persepolis Ruins

23 More Indicted In Election Frauds; Lehman Won't Act

Stimson Acts To Avert War At Leticia; Consults Kellogg Pact Signatories On Colombia Plea Peru Is Aggressor

Britain Bars Trading In Debt Parley In Note Accepting Bid By Roosevelt; House Leaders Move For Tariff Rises

Roosevelt Outlines Plan For Drastic Unifications Under Two New Bureaus

Roosevelt Sets 3 Points In His Economy Program; Cuts In Employes Is One

Ford Is Considering Making Car Bodies

Roosevelt And Lindsey Find A Basis For British Debt 'Meetings' In March, But Envoy Expects Wide Differences

Hitler Made Chancellor Of Germany But Coalition Cabinet Limits Power; Centrists Hold Balance In Reichstag

FEBRUARY

Centrists Demand Hitler Make Clear His Cabinet Policy

Hitler Wins Dissolution Of Reichstag; Urges Nation To End Its 'Humiliation' At Polls March 5; Has 4-Year Plans

Hitler Represses Reds, Puts Curb On Socialists; Pledges Internal Peace

Revolt Of Terror Going On In Cuba; Fear Of Riot Grows

Thousands Forced To Leave Leningrad

Nazi Troops March With Empire Flags As Violence Mounts

Reich Gags Press, Ends Prussian Diet

Roosevelt Invites Governors Mar. 6 To Draft National Recovery Plans; Smith Urges Public Works Dictator

Cold Wave Strikes After Record Warmth; Mercury Falls From 63 to 27 in 8 Hours

Cold Grips Nation, 65 Die; 5-Degree Low Due Here; 11 Missing In The Sound

Hitler Proclaims War On Democracy At Huge Nazi Rally

Japan to Proclaim She Will Not Heed Actions Of League

Dead Slaves Guard Nubian King In Tomb

Hoover Would Let War Debt Be Used To Restore The World To Gold Basis; British Widen Scope Of Debt Talks

Japan Drafts Ultimatum To China To Quit Jehol; League Assembly To Act

Assassin Fires Into Roosevelt Party At Miami; President-Elect Uninjured; Mayor Cermak And 4 Others Wounded

Thankful Crowds Greet Roosevelt, Now Speeding North Unperturbed; Thought Shots Were Firecrackers

League Issues Its Censure Of Japan In 10-Hour Broadcast To The World; Invites U.S. And Russia To Consult

Manchukuo Sends Ultimatum To China; Warns Of Imminent Attack In Jehol; Soong Tells Troops China Will Fight

Germany Is Uneasy About Hindenburg; Fears He Is Weary

House Votes Dry Law Repeal 289-121; States Begin Move For Ratification; Lehman Asks Quick New York Action

Hull And Woodin Named For Cabinet To Speed Action On World Economics; Roosevelt Confers With French Envoy

Tentative List Of Roosevelt Cabinet Includes Miss Perkins Of New York, Ickes, Roper, Dern And Wallace

30,000 Japanese Attack At Chaoyang As China Rejects Tokyo's Ultimatum; Panic In Tientsin; League To Act Today

Japanese Leave The League Assembly After Unanimous Censure By Nations; Tokyo's Troops Seeping On In Jehol

Chaoyang Falls As Japanese Advance; Four Armies And Air Fleet In Drive; Washington Approves League's Action

Ford Takes Over 2 Detroit Banks; Move Ends Tie-Up

Chinese Slow Up Foe In Hard Battle; Say 5,000 Manchukuo Troops Bolted; Britain Bars Export Of Arms To East

MARCH

Japanese Drive Slackens But 2 Armies Make Gains; All North China Is Tense

China's Main Line Broken In Hard Japanese Drive; Chihfeng Troops Desert

Roosevelt In Capital, Will Confer With Hoover Today; Cummings Made Attorney General, Rainey Speaker

Roosevelt Takes Up Task As President Today; Great Crowds In Capital For Inauguration; Extra Session Will Enact A New Bank Policy

Roosevelt Inaugurated, Acts To End The National Banking Crisis Quickly; Will Ask War-Time Powers If Needed

Roosevelt Orders 4-Day Bank Holiday, Puts Embargo On Gold, Calls Congress

Legislature Votes Lehman Wide Bank Powers; Creates A State Corporation To Issue Scrip; Woodin Authorizes New Checking Accounts

Washington Leans To Emergency Currency; Roosevelt Studying 8-Point Bank Program; Banks Here To Furnish Cash For Vital Needs

Roosevelt Gets Pledge Of New Currency Law Today From Congress Chiefs, So Banks Can Open Tomorrow; Scrip Plan Abandoned; Hoarded Gold Is Called Back

Roosevelt Extends The National Banking Holiday; Congress
Empowers Him To Reopen Sound Institutions; Half Billion Budget
Cut Next, Chiefly Veterans' Fund

123 Killed By Earthquake In South California Cities; 4,150 Are
Reported Injured

Earthquake Dead In California 130, Injured 5,000 Loss Over
$45,000,000; Shocks Continue In Long Beach Area

Many Banks In The City And Nation Reopen Today For Normal
Operations, But With Hoarding Barred; Roosevelt Appeals On The
Radio For Full Confidence

Roosevelt Asks For Beer To Provide Needed Revenue; Congress
Speeds Action On This And On Economy Bill; Deposits Exceed
The Withdrawals In Opened Banks

House Votes 3.2 Per Cent Beer, 316-97; Quick Passage By Senate
Forecast; $2,000,000,000 Relief Plan Is Drafted

Senate Passes Economy Bill, 62-13, Barring All But Minor
Amendments; Stocks Soar As Trading Is Resumed

Roosevelt Now Asks Farm Relief; Senate Votes 3.05 Beer And
Wine; $500,000,000 Economy Bill Is Passed

Roosevelt Holds Congress For Rail, Power, Bank Bills; House
Insists On 3.2 Beer

Nazis Order Reich To Celebrate Unity

Mussolini Offers A Plan To Keep European Peace By Revision Of
Treaties

Reichstag Meeting Today Is Prepared To Give Hitler Full Control
As Dictator

Empire Setting Is Revived In New Reichstag Meetings; Hull Asks
Data On Raids

President Signs Bill For Legal Beer; Effective Here At 12:01 A.M.
April 7; House Approves Farm Relief 315-98

Hitler Cabinet Gets Power To Rule As A Dictatorship; Reichstag
Quits Sine Die

Lehman Offers Beer Plan With State Control Board; Old-Time
Bars Forbidden

Germans Aroused By Attacks Abroad; Deny Wide Violence

America in Longest Warm Spell Since 1776; Temperature Line
Records a 25-Year Rise

55,000 Here Stage Protest On Hitler Attacks On Jews; Nazis Order
A New Boycott

Hitlerites Order Boycott Against Jews In Business, Professions And
Schools

Lehman Stirs Legislature In Fight For His Beer Bill; Sees Dry
Repeal In Peril

Lehman Beer Bill Changed, Then Passed By The Senate; Is
Doomed In The Assembly

APRIL

Nazis Cut Boycott To Day With Threat Of Renewal If World Does Not Recant

Nazis Hold 1-Day Boycott; Little Violence In Reich; Resumption Is Unlikely

Lehman Appeals To Public To Free Beer Of Politics; Fearon Retorts On Radio

Dirigible Akron Crashes In Lightning Storm At Sea; Only 4 Of The 77 Men Aboard Are Reported Rescued; Airship Is Believed A Total Loss; Wide Search On

73 Lost In Akron Crash, 3 Survivors Here; Ship Driven Down In Storm, Cause Is Unknown; Rescue Blimp Falls, 2 Killed, 5 Are Saved

Beer Is Legal At Midnight; Brewers To Ban 'Carnival'; State Repeal Vote May 23

Beer Flows In 19 States At Midnight As City Awaits Legal Brew Today; 3.2 Era Opens Here With Few Revels

Nation Has Beer Shortage; 1,000,000 Barrels Consumed; Rush Brings In Big Revenue

Roosevelt Scraps Policy Of Economic Nationalism To Assist World Parley

Negro Found Guilty In Scottsboro Case; Jury Out 22 Hours

Negroes in Riotous March on Broadway Welcome Defender in the Scottsboro Case

Schwarz Ousted As Reich Consul; Assails Hitler

Roosevelt Savings Reach $1,020,000,000 In 1934 Outlay; Campaign Pledge Exceeded

Roosevelt Advisers Draft Plan To Mobilize Industry; Tariff Dictatorship Looms

Anti-Jewish 'Drive' Is Staged In Tokyo

Soviet 'Frame-Up' Charged By Briton At Moscow Trial

Britons' Expulsion After Soviet Trial Held To Be Likely

Senate Rejects 16-1 Silver As A Clause In Farm Bill; Inflationists Get 33 Votes

Roosevelt To Halt All Gold Export; Plans More Liberal Reserve Credit; Industry Control Being Worked Out

Gold Standard Dropped For The Present To Lift Prices And Aid Our Trade Position; Plans For Controlled Inflation Drafted

Senate Gets Bill For Controlled Inflation Making The President Monetary Dictator; Stocks And Commodities Continue To Soar

Roosevelt Confers With M'Donald On Economic Recovery Of World; Republicans Attack Inflation Bill

Roosevelt And M'Donald Favor World Action On Money And Trade; Bitter Inflation Fight In Senate

Exchange Agreement Near, Experts Tell White House; Herriot Arrives For Talks

Roosevelt And M'Donald In Harmony On London Economic Parley Policies; Herriot Starts White House Talks

Roosevelt And M'Donald Report A 'Clearer Understanding' On Debt; Economic Parley To Open June 12

Roosevelt Seeks Debt-Tariff Deals, World Money Basis; Aids Disarming; Senate Votes Free Silver Proposal

Senate Votes 53-35 To Cut Gold Content Of Dollar; Herriot For Tariff Truce

Senate Passes Inflation-Farm Bill By 64-20; Industry Control Bill Permits Price Fixing; Three Nations To Act To Stabilize Exchange

Trade Deal With Canada Looms As Result Of Talks; Davis Offers Tariff Truce

MAY

Gandhi Plans Fast Lasting 3 Weeks

Hitler Will Draft Youth For Labor; 1,000,000 Hail Him

Nazis Seize Unions And Arrest Chiefs; Plan One Big Body

Inflation Bill Adopted In the House By 307-86; 30 Republicans
Back It

Roosevelt Asks Pay Rise For Workers; Promises To Help Business
End Chaos; He Sends Railroad Bill To Congress

Kidnapped Girl Is Found On A Boat Near Her Home; Ransom Of
$80,000 Paid

Kidnappers Seized, $60,000 Recovered; Child Aids Police

Roosevelt Promises A 'Partnership' With Business, Farmers And
Workers To Provide Profits And Higher Wages

President Expected To Get Right To Act On War Debts During
Recess Of Congress

Britain Agrees To A Tariff Truce; Roosevlet To Ask Bargaining
Power; Davis Warns Berlin On Arms Stand

Nazi Book-Burning Fails To Stir Berlin

Paris Now Offers To Pay Dec. 15 Debt If We Agree To Holiday
During Parley

Hitler Calls Reichstag On Arms Issue; France Declares Opposition
To Nazis; Eight Nations Approve Tariff Truce

Europe Anxiously Awaits Hitler Arms Declaration; Isolation
Disturbs Reich

Nazi Leaders Now Uneasy Over Hostility Of World; Davis
Working For Accord

Roosevelt To Outline Foreign Policy In Statement To The World
Today; Nazis Face United Opponents On Arms

Roosevelt Asks Peace Through Arms Cuts In A Plea To 54 Nations,
Including Russia; He Proposes A New Pact Of Non-Aggression

Hitler Says Reich Will Forego Arms But Will No Longer Remain
Inferior; Roosevelt Plans Other Peace Steps

Hugh S. Johnson Chosen 'Dictator' Of Industry; Four Tax Plans
Offered

Harriman Vanishes; Police Speed Hunt To Avert Suicide

Harriman Stabs Himself As He Is Found In Roslyn; His Wounds
Not Serious

4 Powers Agree At Rome To Keep Peace Ten Years; France Shifts
Arms Policy

Davis Pledges US To Consult On War And Not Block Action On
Aggressor; London Now Sees Success Of Parleys

Morgan Paid No Income Tax For The Years 1931 And 1932;
Neither Did His Partners

Morgan Stock Favor List Revealed; Woodin, Adams, M'Adoo,
Young On It; Move Is Started To Change Tax Laws

Morgan Foreign Financing Detailed, Fees Disclosed; Coolidge On
One Stock List

Gold Clause Repeal Asked By Roosevelt To Permit Payments In
Legal Tender

Gen. Feng Rebels To Fight Japanese And Depose Chiang

Austria To Fight Nazis To A Finish, Dollfuss Asserts

Roosevelt To Act On Debts; May Waive June Interest; House Votes
Gold Repeal

Germany Rejects Report To League That Her Laws Violate Silesian
Treaty

JUNE

Morgan Favor Recipients Held To Share Stock Risk; Senator Kean
On New List

Hitler To Expand Credit In His Recovery Program; Subsidies For
Marriages

City Agrees On New Taxes On Bridges And Taxicabs; Real Estate
Fees Raised

Roosevelt Urged To Veto Senate Veteran Increases To Save
Economy Program

Roosevelt Warns House Leaders They Must Levy $170,675,067
Taxes If They Restore Veteran Pensions

Mattern Flies For Omsk; Beats Record To Moscow After Landing
Near Oslo

Aldermen Vote Auto Tax As City Wide Fight Begins; Legality Is
Challenged

Roosevelt Trims Program To Hasten End Of Session; Sees His
Policies Menaced

Banks Renew City Loans To Dec. 11 At Rate Of 5 3/4% On
$30,000,000 Tax Pledge

Morgan Defends His Taxes, Stock Lists And Business; Senators Hear Partners

Senators Plan To Adjourn By Filibuster On Reorganization; House Completes Action On Bills

Trade Parley Opens Today In Move To Speed Recovery; Monetary Truce Is Sought

Roosevelt Threatens Veto And Appeal To The Nation If Senate Voids Economies

Senate Fight On Veterans Again Halts Adjournment; Industrial Bill Is Passed

Britain Pays US $10,000,000 In Silver, Asks Revision; Roosevelt Bars Debt Action At Economic Conference; Senate Passes Veteran Amendment, Courting Veto

London Parley Draws Plan For Stabilized Currencies; Woodin Denies Agreement

President Starts Recovery Program, Signs Bank, Rail And Industry Bills; Wheat Growers Will Get $150,000,000

5 Slain In Battle By Gang To Free Oklahoma Bandit

Parley In Dilemma As Americans Fail To Clarify Policies

Our Domestic Recovery Put First By Washington; London Turning To Prices

10 Nations Outline Price Problems; First Parley Test Coming On Wheat; Moley Flies to Consult Roosevelt

1,629,000 New Jobs Created In Nation In Past 2 Months

Hitler Ousts Socialists From Reichstag And Diets; Suppresses Their Party

Conference Is Handicapped By Indecision Over Policies, But MacDonald Is Hopeful

Hull Pushes Plans to Raise Prices; First Accord Likely On Wheat Cuts; Fight On Labor In Industry Seen Here

Life Is Merely Dreamed, New Nerve Theory Holds

Freer Use Of Silver Money Gaining Support In London; Couzens Urges Price Rises

25% Gold Reserve Enough, Parley's Experts Decide; Britain Won't Peg Pound

French Seek Aid For Franc To Avert Devalorization; Moley Sees Recovery Here

Europe Asks Roosevelt Aid To End Dollar Speculation, Called Menace To Parley

JULY

Federal Reserves To 'Steady' Dollar, Easing Fluctuations During Parley; Roosevelt Permits Actions By Banks

Roosevelt Bars Gold Pact In Form Proposed By Bloc; Meets Cabinet Tomorrow

$4,000,000 Lent To Soviet By R.F.C. To Buy Cotton; Other Loans Are Expected

Roosevelt Rebuke Stuns Gold Bloc, But Conference Is Likely To Go On; President Turns To Domestic Drive

Roosevelt Sends Message Instructing Our Delegates To Keep Conference Going

London Conference Ready To Recess Today, Probably To October, On Gold Bloc's Demand; Roosevelt To Base Dollar On 1924-25 Prices

Hull Plea Saves London Conference; All Factions Work On New Agenda; Roosevelt Pressing Home Recovery

Roosevelt Drafts Message Detailing Plan For Parley To Increase World Prices

Roosevelt Asks Alabama To Vote Dry Law Repeal As A Democratic Pledge

Hitler Seeks Jobs For All Germans

J.J. O'Connell Jr. Seized By Kidnappers In Albany; $250,000 Ransom Sought

O'Connells Name New Negotiators In Ransom Demand

Roosevelt Orders Farley To Place All Postmasters Under The Civil Service

Rush Of Industry Codes Swamps Recovery Board; Coal And Oil Leaders Act

President Considers Order Fixing Wages And Hours, Pending Code Agreements

Steel Code Grants Pay Rise Of 15% To Skilled Workers; 40-Hour Week Is Proposed

Post In Berlin In 25 3/4 Hours; Delayed In East Prussia By Storms, Then Flies On

1,000,000 Begin Short Week, Or Receive Higher Wages, As 'New Deal' Functions

Repeal Wins In Alabama And Arkansas By 3 To 2; Large Wet Vote In Cities

Great Italian Air Armada Is Acclaimed By Millions As It Wings Over The City

Post, Lost, lands In Alaska Village; Plane Is Damaged

Peek Calls Parley Monday To Curb Grain Speculation; President Watches Stocks

Post Arrives Safely In New York, Circling World In 7 Days, 19 Hours; Mollisons Are Flying The Atlantic

Mollisons Crash At Bridgeport; Both Are Injured, Planes Wrecked; Had Flown From Wales In 39 Hours

Roosevelt Appeals To The Nation For Unified Action To Spur Recovery; Peek Demands Grain Trading Reform

Nation Pledges Support To The President's Code In A Flood Of Messages

President Starts Mobilizing Nation For 6,000,000 Jobs

Lehman Acts To Put State Behind The Recovery Drive; Rush Of Employers To Sign

NRA To Leave Pay In Higher Scales To The Employer

11 New York Banks Pledge Help To NRA By Financing The Production Of Goods

Kidnappers Free O'Connell After Payment Of $40,000; Thinks He Was Held Here

AUGUST

Death For Kidnappers, With Ransoming A Felony, Is Demanded
By Lehman

Mob Stops Train Seeking 3 Lawyers

14,000 Banks Adopt Code Covering Hours And Pay; NRA Acts In
Coal Strike

NRA Makes New Move To Settle Coal Strike; Roosevelt In Touch

Gas Bombs Shut Stock Exchange; 4 Suspects Held

Roosevelt Appoints Board Of 7 To Decide All Disputes Over
Industrial Problems

Government Will Adjust Its Contracts Under NRA To Meet Cost
Increases

Havana Police Kill Score In Crowd Outside Capitol; Machado
Expected To Quit

Gunmen Try To Kill Politician In Home

Roosevelt Calls On Cuba To Drop Political Strife; Island Under
Martial Law

Machado Drafts A Formula Countering Welles's Plan; Strikers
Refuse To Return

Cuban Army Rises Against Machado; Demands He Resign By Noon Today; Roosevelt Studies Reconstruction

Machado Flies to A Secret Refuge; De Cespedes Made President Of Cuba; 18 Killed As Mobs Avenge Murders

Roosevelt Sends Warships To Cuba To Guard Americans, Not Intervene; De Cespedes Sworn In; Riots Subside

China Flood Covers 10,000 Square Miles

Rackets Linked To Politics By Medalie And Kernochan; Gang Escapes Police Trap

Roosevelt Ready To Act In Steel And Coal Tangle By Drafting Their Codes

Johnson Drafts Oil Code, Demands Action On Coal; Seeks New Chiefs For NRA

Steel Agreement Reached, Wins President's Approval; Average 40-Hour Week Set

Roosevelt Approves Codes For Steel, Oil And Lumber; Coal Groups Still Debate

Reich Fails To Gain Under Nazis' Rule; Foes Are Helpless

NRA Drafting Coal Code; Compact On Autos Near; Retail Hearing On Today

Johnson Seeks Federal Aid To Finance NRA Industries; Says Banks Lag In Credits

Johnson Will Not Permit Use Of Term 'Open Shop' In Code Of Any Industry

Roosevelt Gets Coal Men And Union Heads To Confer; Price Fixing In Retail Code

21 Nations In Wheat Pact, Curb Output And Exports; Inflation Issue Is Shelved

Roosevelt Sees The Nation Started On Upward Surge; Calls Policy Permanent

Moley Resigns From Post To Edit A New Magazine Backed By Vincent Astor

RFC Told By President To Seek Credits For NRA; Coal Agreement Reached

Exportation Of Mine Gold Permitted By Roosevelt; Time Limit For Hoarders

$37,500,000 Loan To City For 38th Street Tunnel; 4-Year Job For 8,000 Men

SEPTEMBER

Johnson Aide Resigns In Clash On NRA Policy; Labor Issue Still Active

Nazis Pledge Jobs; Hitler Places Art On A 'Nordic' Basis

Hitler Sees Reich Nazi For All Time; Aides Assail Jews

Hitler Disclaims Desire For A War; 150,000 In Review

Cuban Troops Rise Against Officers; Rule By Committee

Radical Junta Rules Cuba As Army Ousts Cespedes; We Rush 4 Warships There

We Consult Latin America As Swanson Goes To Cuba; Wells Reports 'Disquiet'

29 U.S. Ships On Cuban Duty; Factions There Adopt Plan For Nation To Save Itself

Cubans Seeks A Coalition As Army Crisis Continues; Mexico Pleads For Order

Cuba's Rebel Junta Yields To Demand For President; Plans to Hold Elections

Grau San Martin Sworn In As Cuba's New President; Army Officers Are Defiant

O'Brien To Push Tax Plan Despite Stormy Protest; Rejects Savings Bank Aid

Johnson Tells NRA Rally Depression Is 25% Lifted By Roosevelt's Program

1,500,000 Cheer Vast NRA Parade; March Of 250,000 City's Greatest; Demonstration Lasts Till Midnight

Coal Men Tell Roosevelt Code Will Be Signed Today; 16 Shot In Riots At Mines

Soft Coal Code Approved By Operators And Miners; Wage Agreements Near

Operators Accept Code For Soft Coal Industry; Union To Be Recognized

Lehman Ready To Step In As Banks Ask He Be Called To Help Solve City Crisis

President Refuses To Resign In Cuba; Dictatorship Seen

Prial Defeats Tammany By 70,000; O'Brien And Rest Of Slate Victors; Koenig Defeat By Mellen Indicated

7 Gangsters Seized Here In O'Connell Kidnapping; Linked To Five Murders

President Orders Outlay Of $75,000,000 To Clothe And Feed The Unemployed

Roosevelt Offers To Lend 10 Cent A Pound On Cotton To Farmers Reducing Crops

Austria To Set Up Nazi Prison Camps

M'Kee To Run, Farley Says; Aides Pick Running Mate; Untermyer Hits Pay Cut

Tampico In Ruins; Hundreds Killed In 150-Mile Gale

O'Brien Vetoes Stock Tax; Exchange Decides To Stay; New Payroll Crisis Near

Banks Agree To City Finance Plan; Lehman Breaks Deadlock In Crisis; M'Kee To Make Statement Today

City Accepts Four-Year Credit Plan; Vote 10% Tax Penalty; Loans At 4%; M'Kee Now Is Expected Not To Run

M'Kee In Race, Denounces 'Corrupt, Stupid' Tammany; Curry And Fusion Worried

OCTOBER

Roosevelt Decides To Buy Coal, Food And Clothing For The Needy This Winter

Buy Now Campaign Without Ballyhoo Begins Next Week

Heavy Fighting In Havana; 119 Dead, One An American; Officers Surrender Hotel

Dollfuss Is Shot By Austrian Nazi

Briton Denounces Nazi Racial Views At Geneva Session

Pecora On M'Kee's Ticket; Bronx Breaks With Curry; Leaders Face Loss Of Jobs

M'Kee Refuses M'Naboe Aid; Fertig Quits Curry Ticket; Goldman Ousted, 200 To Go

President Orders Accord At Once On Captive Mines, Or He Will Act Himself

Hillquit, Leader Of Socialists, Dies

Democrats Bolt To M'Kee In Brooklyn And Queens; A Job Rush, Seabury Says

M'Cooey Rule Collapsing As Leaders Go To M'Kee; O'Brien Opens His Campaign

M'Kee Opens His Campaign; Denies Control By 'Boss'; Would
End Needless Jobs

Lone Island Picked To Imprison Worst Of Our Criminals

A.F. Of L. Votes A Boycott On All German Products Until
Persecution Ceases

Germany Quits League And Arms Parley; Hitler Scores Treaty,
Demands Equality; Call Election Nov. 12 To Obtain Approval

Brief Arms Parley Recess Sought In Move To Save It; Note To Be
Sent To Reich

M'Kee Denounces Race Bias Charge; Cites His Record

Bosses Denounced By Prial At Rally In Tammany Hall; O'Brien
Gets An Ovation

Hitler Rejects Parleys Till Equality Is Granted; Acts To Win Foes At
Home

M'Kee Charges Tammany With Relief Fund Graft; Mills Speaks
For Fusion

Roosevelt Acts To Recognize Russia With Invitation To Conference
Here; Litvinoff Coming To Discuss Issues

O'Brien Prohibits Celebration Here Of German Society

Roosevelt Announces New Policy To Value Dollar; To Fix Price Of
Gold After Putting Up Commodities; Answers Critics Of The NRA
In Radio Talk To Nation

Roosevelt Will Buy Gold At Once Above World Price; Stocks Rise;
Code For Retail Stores Is Signed

Gold Buying Starts Today; Price Will Be Fixed Daily; NRA Import Curb Studied

Gold Buying Opens At $31.36 Only 27c Over World Price

M'Kee Outlines Program, Listing 21 Major Planks; Seabury Attack Record

President Declares Ford Ineligible For Contracts Under Provisions Of NRA

Arabs Riot Again; Palestine Unrest Spreading Outside

Roosevelt Decides To Buy Gold In World's Markets; RFC Will Make Purchases

2,500 In Mob Raid Detroit Die Plants

NOVEMBER

LaGuardia And M'Kee Agree Economy Can Slash Budget; 4-Year Bank Plan Is Signed

Nazis Swallow Up Ullstein Press, Largest In Reich

Fusion Candidates Cheered At Great Rally In Garden; Farley To Vote For M'Kee

Governors Draft A Plan For Drastic Price Fixing; President May Modify It

Rival Parties Stage Big Rallies As City Campaign Nears Its Close; All Leaders Speak In Final Drive

Three Parties See Victory In Tomorrow's Election; Managers Make Forecasts

Huge City Vote Is Expected Today; All Candidates Fight To Very End; M'Kee Sees Election Fraud Plot

LaGuardia Elected Mayor Of New York; Fusion Controls Board Of Estimate; Repeal Of 18th Amendment Is Assured

Capacity Liquor Output Permitted By Roosevelt; Repeal Effective Dec. 5

State Liquor Rules Issued; Old-Time Saloon Banned; Rigid Curbs On Retail Sale

Hitler Stops All Industry an Hour For Final Plea for Unanimous Vote

HIndenburg Urges 100% Hitler Vote

40,618,147 For Hitler In Record German Poll; 2,055,363 'Noes' Counted

Nazis Look Abroad For The Next Step; Hitler Hides Plans

'Mr. X' At Hearing Details Nazi 'Plot'

W.K. Vanderbilt Jr. Is Killed In South; His Car Hits Truck

Nazi Church Laws to Be Revoked; 'Non-Aryans' Now Acceptable

United States Recognizes Soviet, Exacting Pledge On Propaganda; Bullitt Named First Ambassador

Roosevelt Scores 'Tories' And 'Doubting Thomases'; Sees Peace In Soviet Pact

Protestants Balk At Curb By Nazis; Condemn 'Pagans'

A.A.U. Boycotts 1936 Olympics Because Of the Nazi Ban On Jews

Sprague Quits Treasury To Attack Gold Policy; Roosevelt Going Ahead

Reserve's Advisers Urge We Return To Gold Basis; President Hits At 'Foes'

End Of Dollar Uncertainty Expected Soon in Capital; RFC Gold Price Unchanged

Roosevelt Won't Change Government's Gold Policy, Ignoring
Attack By Smith

Hitler Asks New Accord Ending Versailles Pact; Consults French
Envoy

6,000 Watch A Mob Hang Slayers Of Brooke Hart As Body Is
Found In Bay

President Brings Movies And Liquor Under NRA Rule

Missouri Negro, 19, Lynched, Despite Soldiers And Tanks; Troops
Win Maryland Fight

Four In Maryland Held As Lynchers Freed By Court

DECEMBER

Royal Bones Convict Richard III Of Murders in the Tower in 1483

Waxey Gordon Guilty; Gets 10 Years, Is Fined $80,000 For Tax Evasion

Swanson Warns Of 'Impaired' Navy As Inviting War

Spain Moves to Crush Disorders As Right Parties Gain in Election

Legal Liquor Due Tonight; City Ready To Celebrate; Stores To Open Tomorrow

Prohibition Repeal Is Ratified At 5:32 P.M.; Roosevelt Asks Nation To Bar The Saloon; New York Celebrates With Quiet Restraint

Liquor For Homes Scarce; Speakeasy Raids Go On; Inquiry On Prices Likely

Britain Is Unmoved By Mussolini Plan To Reform League

Roosevelt Calls On Peek To Head Bureau To Seek Liquor Import Treaties

Spain Crushes Anarchist Rebels; 42 Killed, Hundreds Wounded

Anarchists Renew Uprising In Spain; Madrid Is Bombed

High Liquor Tax Barred By Roosevelt In Order To Destroy
Bootlegger

3 Stowaways Found on Byrd Ship; Add to Problem of
Overcrowding

Berle, Moses, Blanshard In The LaGuardia Cabinet; 3 Other
Liberals Chosen

NRA Warns Weir Not To Break Law; Steel Man Defiant

Morgenthau Asks Revision To Close Income Tax Gaps; For Low
Rate Under $25,000

Dr. Einstein Doubts Light Speed Varies

U.S. Move To Block A Feminism Treaty Laid To Strife Here

RFC Seeks A Billion More To Lend To Closed Banks; Wants Added
Year Of Life

City Orders A New Label On All Whisky By Jan. 5, Showing The
Ingredients

400,000 Germans To Be Sterilized

President Orders Purchase of 24,421,410 Silver Ounces Yearly, Half
To Be Coined

Van Der Lubbe Gets Sentence Of Death, Four Others Freed

Sterilization Condemned by Pope; Nazis' Plan Is Held UnChristian

Archbishop Assassinated In Procession To Altar; Laid To Old-World
Feud

City Yuletide Gay, All The Needy Fed; Less Intoxication

Roosevelt Busy Drafting Plans For New Congress; He Consults Many Aides

Stalin Says Japan Is 'Grave Danger'; Hopes For Peace

New Cooperation Policy For Western Hemisphere Outlined By Roosevelt

Mercury 3 Below Zero, Coldest Day In 14 Years; Relief Here Due Today

Cold Wave Ends In City After Dip To 6 Below Zero

1934: NEW YORK TIMES (365)

JANUARY

First New Year's Revel Since Repeal Is Orderly; The Gayest In 14 Years

LaGuardia Moves To Clean Up City; Starts Hunt For Graft In Bureaus; Tammany Organizes The Aldermen

LaGuardia Asks Albany To Give Him Full Power Over The City's Finances

'New Deal' Is Here To Stay, President Tells Congress; Sees Recovery Under Way

Roosevelt Spending $10,569,006,967 To June 30; New Borrowing 6 Billion, Plus 4 Billion To Retire Maturities

Lehman Warns LaGuardia He Asks Too Much Power; Rejects A 'Dictatorship'

LaGuardia Ready To Fight For Powers Of Dictator; Drafts Reply To Lehman

LaGuardia Tells Lehman He Plans No Dictatorship; Decries 'Political' Move

Gov. Lehman Again Rejects LaGuardia 'Dictator' Plan; Invites Mayor To Confer

Postal Records Burned On Orders Of Secretary Of Brown, Clerk
Swears

Lehman And Mayor Agree On Economy Bill Granting Power To
Estimate Board

Roosevelt Forces Crush Economy Revolt In House; Gold Profit
Plan Studied

Roosevelt Claims Power To Capture Reserve Bank Gold

President Confers Tonight With Congress Committees On His
Monetary Program

President Will Ask Power To Take All Monetary Gold As Step To
Revalue Dollar

President Plans 50 To 60-Cent Dollar And $2,000,000,000
Equalization Fund From Profit On Impounding Of Gold

Hostile Tammany Forces Resist LaGuardia's Bill In Both Albany
Chambers

Gold Bill Constitutional, Cummings Tells Senate; Early Passage
Expected

Byrd Arrives at Little America; Amazed by Vast Upheaval of Ice

Steingut Sees President, Promises To Aid Lehman Pass City
Economy Bill

House Passes Gold Bill, 360-40 Rejecting Changes; New Financing
Taken Up

Germans Flout League As Nazi Tide Threatens Austria, Saar And
Danzig

Time Limit On Gold Bill Is Urged By Owen D. Young; Support
For It In Senate

Treasury Asks $1,000,000,000 Through Usual Methods; Senate
Gets The Gold Bill

Welfare Island Raid Bares Gangster Rule Over Prison; Weapons,
Narcotics Found

Change In City Bill Looms As Workers Fight Pays Slashes

Reich And Poland Sign A Peace Pact

Grave Crisis In France As Government Resigns Over Bank Scandal
Riots

Nazis Ease Budget By Forced 'Gifts' To Party Treasury

LaGuardia's Bill Fought By Assembly Democrats; Lehman
Demands Action

Nation Honors President At 6,000 Birthday Dinners; He Voices
Sincere Thanks

FEBRUARY

Britain And Italy Offer Two Plans To Rearm Reich

Washington Acts To Avert Exchange War On Dollar; Stocks Rise, Bank Rate Cut

W.P. M'Cracken Arrested By Order Of The Senate In Air Mail Investigation

Taxi Strikers Seize Cabs, Rip Off Doors And Force Theatre Crowds To Walk

Taxi Strike Is Settled As LaGuardia Intervenes; Extra Fare To Be Divided

LaGuardia Asks Taxi Code As Men Reject Settlement; Hotel Pickets Fight Police

Shouting Mobs Riot All Night In Paris, Storm Chamber, Demand Government Resign; Police Fire At Them; 10 Killed, 500 Injured

Riots Subside As Daladier Quits And Doumergue Is Called To Paris; Strong Non-Party Cabinet Planned

Kidnappers Free Bremer On Payment Of $200,000; Wide Manhunt Is Pushed

Air Contracts Canceled; Army To Carry The Mails; M'Cracken Evades Arrest

M'Cracken Stays In Home Of Senate Officer As Offer To Surrender Is Rejected

Nazi State Fights Catholic Church To Curb Its Power

129 Austrians Killed In Civil War; Socialists Declare General Strike; Dollfuss Bans Party; Nazis Lie Low

Government Is Winning In Austria; Socialists Fight On, Hundreds Dead; Model Vienna Apartments Shelled

Socialists Renew Fighting After Retreat In Vienna; Dollfuss Offers Amnesty

Brown Denies Mail Deals Involved Any Illegality; He Will Testify Monday

Vienna Quiet Again; Nazis Woo Rebels

King Albert Falls To Death Climbing Peak Near Namur; Body Found, Wound In Head

King's Death Stuns Belgium; State Funeral Thursday; Fell Climbing Peak Alone

Vast Crowds In Brussels Bow Before King's Coffin As Body Reaches Palace

9-Inch Snow Cripples City; Suburbs Cut Off For Hours; Travel Hit In Whole East

50,000 Dig City Out; Many In Suburbs Still Snowbound

King Albert Laid To Rest By Sorrowful Belgium; His Son Takes Oath Today

Leopold Ascends Belgian Throne; Pledge to Serve Nation Cheered

House Votes Air Mail Bill After Acrimonious Debate; Farley Contradicts Brown

9 Dartmouth Students Die In Fraternity House From Monoxide Poisoning

City Battles 9-Inch Snow; Rail Tie-Up Maroons Towns; Zero Cold Is Likely Today

Johnson Meets NRA Critics, Proposes 12-Point Revision; J.W. Davis Scores New Deal

MARCH

Pu Yi Ascends Throne Of Manchukuo Empire In Centuries-Old Ritual

Roosevelt Asks Free Hand On Money In Coming Year; New Labor Plan In Senate

Roosevelt Offers Philippines Plan, Removing Army

Dillinger Escapes Jail; Using A Wooden Pistol He Locks Guards In Cell

Dillinger Eludes Hunt In 4 States; 'Kill' Order Issued

New Deal Permanent, President Says; Asks Higher Pay, Shorter Hours, Now; Supreme Court Upholds Price Fixing

Code Delegates Hesitate To Cut Hour, Raise Pay, Without Price Increases

Roosevelt Urges Return Of Mails To Air Companies Under Strict Safeguards

Tariff Rule By Roosevelt To Aid Foreign Trade Asked By Hull, Wallace And Roper

Roosevelt Will Suspend Liquor Quotas To Reduce Prices, End Bootlegging

President Orders The Army To Fly Mail Only On Routes That Don't Imperil Fliers

Army Grounds Mail Planes To Wait For New Schedules; 20% Further Cut Forecast

House Votes Bonus, 295-125, After Disorderly Debate; Defeat In Senate Expected

Manny Strewl Convicted Of Kidnapping O'Connell; Banghart Gets 99 Years

Air Inquiry Post Declined Sharply By Col. Lindbergh

Samuel Insull Vanishes; Greeks Start Wide Hunt; Cabinet Crisis Expected

Lindbergh Assails Air Mail Measure Before Senators

5,000 Fight Police In Harlem Streets

Mussolini Urges German Rearming To Avoid Disaster

12 Industrial Credit Banks Sought In Roosevelt Bill; Silver Bloc Wins In House

President Wins Auto Strike Delay; Rail Managers Accept His Pay Truce; Trade Board Assails NRA Steel Code

Roosevelt Hears Case Of Auto Manufacturers; Rail Men Will Arbitrate

Police Quell Taxi Rioters In Sharp Times Sq. Battle After A Day Of Violence

Settlement Of Auto Strife Expected To Be Announced By The
President Today

Premier Warns France To End Civil War Threat; Sees Danger Of
Invasion

Violence Renewed By Taxi Strikers Who Reject Poll

Roosevelt Wants 'Teeth' In Stock Exchange Bill; Seeks Speculation
Limit

House, 310 To 72, Overrides Roosevelt's Veteran Veto; Close Senate
Vote Likely

Senate Overrides Veterans Veto, Crippling Whole Economy
Program; 29 Democrats Desert The President

State Senator's Letters Indicate Associated Gas Paid For Political
Work

Wide Inquiry On Utilities To Be Demanded In Albany; Move To
Impeach Thayer

APRIL

Dillinger Shoots Way Out Of Trap

Turkish Cabinet Decides To Give Up Insull To U.S. After Hearing In Court

Wide Public Utility Inquiry Sought In The Legislature; Thayer Offers Explanation

4 1/4 Liberties Refunded At 3 1/4 In New Treasury Financing; Record Set By State Bonds

Hitler Lieutenant Refuses Bid As Harvard Commencement Aide

Assembly Votes City Bill; Drastic Curbs On Mayor; Lehman Utility Plan Upset

Rioting Minneapolis Mob Forces Council To Yield To Demands For Relief

Two Norwegian Towns Engulfed By Waves as Cliff Falls Into Sea

Fists Fly At Rally Of 9,000 Nazis Here

NRA Settles Motor Strike, Workers Getting 10% Rise; Johnson Goes To Roosevelt

Wirt Names 'Satellites' Of Brain Trust As Source Of His Revolution Story

Wide Inquiry On Utilities Voted By Albany Senate; Thayer Examiner Named

Bar Acts To Oust Justice Kunstler; Calls Him Corrupt

Senate Passes The Tax Bill To Raise $481,000,000 More; President Welcomed Back

Russia And Italy Slash Payrolls In Economy Wave

President To Ask Congress To Vote $1,500,000,000 Relief; Seeks Adjournment May 15

Authenticity Of Letters Is Admitted By Thayer; Stock Deal Profits Told

Japan Warns Powers on China; Threatens Force to Put End to Aid

Paris Breaks Off Arms Talks, Asking Return To Geneva

Curry Foes Confident Of Ousting Him Today; He Pins Hope On Hines

Tammany Ousts Curry, 14 1/3 To 10 1/6; He Accuses Allies Of Disloyalty; Steering Committee To Be Named

Roosevelt Men To Guide Tammany On Leadership; Party Harmony The Aim

Dillinger Is Surrounded In A Forest In Wisconsin; National Guard Called

Dillinger Escapes Posses After Two Running Fights; Two Killed, Five Wounded

Roosevelt Chides Nation For Not 'Thinking Ahead'; Scores 30-Day Panceas

Machado Is Hunted Here On Extradition Warrant; Murder Charged In Cuba

Radium Is Found in Thunderstorms, Drawn From Earth and Rained Back

City Charter Revision Bill Voted As Legislature Closes In Rumpus; Drinking At Bars Is Also Enacted

Choate Finds Bootlegger Is Active Despite Repeal; Illicit Output Colossal

Berlin Is Jammed For May Day Fete; 2,000,000 To March

MAY

Our Envoy Informs Japan We Desire Treaties Be Kept; Affirms Our Rights In China

4,000 Reds In Barricades Defy The Police In Paris; New York May Day Quiet

Johnson Plans New Drive To Revive Interest In NRA; Not To Rely On Penalties

'Time To Stop Crying Wolf,' Roosevelt Tells Chamber; Asks Cooperation Instead

Gunmen Kill Policeman, Shoot Down Two Other And Wound 4 Civilians

Cunningham Dies; Fusion's Control In City Menaced

Germany Now Submits Traveler To Thorough Search on Leaving

Britain Opens Trade War On Japanese In Colonies; Cuts Textile Buying 57%

Nazis Free Fault-Finding Editor; Allow the Press Limited Liberty

M'Goldrick Made City Controller; Long Tammany Foe

Large Banks Plan To Pay Depositors In Harriman And Settle Federal Suit

Huge Dust Cloud, Blown 1,500 Miles, Dims City 5 Hours

Pier Men Quit Here; Mobs On Coast Riot

Gettle Is Hunted In Gang Hideouts Of Los Angeles

Robles Girl And Gettle Safe Home; Child Chained In Pit Under Cactus; Six Seized As Gettle's Kidnappers

Three Gettle Kidnappers Sentenced To Life Terms On Quick Pleas Of Guilty

Silver Program Decided, Adding Metal To Reserve At President's Discretion

President To Ask Congress For Far-Reaching Reforms, Both Social And Economic

Roosevelt Asks Control Of Arms, Chaco Embargo; British Speed Air Defense

Bulgaria Turns Fascist In Coup Aided By The King; Socialist Leaders Seized

Darrow Board Finds NRA Tends Toward Monopoly; Johnson Condemns Report

Mob Of 1,000 Raids Jersey Nazi Rally

President Asks Silver Base Be 'Ultimately' 1 To 3 Gold; Wants 50% Speculation Tax

Barrow And Woman Are Slain By Police In Louisiana Trap

Two Slain, Score Injured, As National Guard Fires On Toledo Strike Rioters

Nazis' Left Pushes Anti-Rich Crusade

Exchange Bill Agreement Provides New 5-Man Board, Flexible Curb On Margins

Roosevelt Ends Regulation Of The Service Industries, But Keeps Code Labor Rule

Roosevelt Bars The Sale Of Arms To Foes In Chaco In Move To Stop Warfare

U.S. Court Refuses To Enjoin Weirton On Labor Election; Reverse For NRA And Unions

Roosevelt Hails New Unity In Nation In Gettysburg Battlefield Speech; Reaches City To Review Fleet Today

JUNE

President Reviews Great Naval Pageant; 81 Warships, 185 Planes Sweep Up The Bay, Thrilling City Throngs With Might Of Fleet

Throngs Flock To Fleet As City Welcomes Navy; 100,000 Are Turned Away

Relief Bill Gives President Funds Netting $6,000,000,000; He Acts At Once On Drought

125,000 Board The Fleet, While As Many More Fail; 2 Drown, 38 Prostrated

British 'Suspend' Payments Pending War Debt Revision; Note Denies Repudiation

Dr. Luther Accused In Inquiry On Nazis

Roosevelt Denies Danger Of Famine In Crop Disaster

Large Corporations Rush To Reorganize On Terms Of New Bankruptcy Law

Roosevelt Sets Security For Homes, Jobs, Old Age As New Deal's Objectives

Berlin Suspends Payment 2 Weeks On French Trade

Wide Hunt Nets No Trace Of Plane With 7 Aboard; Feared Smashed On Peak

Plane Found With 7 Dead On A Peak In Catskills; Crashed In Woods In Fog

Hull Proposes To Britain Debt Payments In Goods; Lays Basis For Negotiation

Peek Shows 22 Billion Loss For US In Foreign Accounts; Asserts We Must Buy More

Reich Suspends Payments On All Its Foreign Debts; British Retaliation Likely

Il Duce And Hitler Agree On Freedom For Austria; Oppose Rival Ententes

Drive To Adjourn The Congress Fails As Senate Recesses Until Tomorrow; Roosevelt Labor Compromise Voted

14 Killed, 60 Hurt As Radicals Shoot At Havana Parade

Congress Adjourns Sine Die After Voting Housing Bill; Helps Labor And Farmers

Hindenburg Backs Papen In Nazi Cabinet Dispute; Move For Monarchy Seen

Liner Dresden Wrecked On A Rock Off Norway; 4 Die As Panic Grips 980

Anti-Nazis Break Into Harvard Yard

Reich Limits Purchases To Daily Foreign Income As Trade War Threatens

U.S. Offers $10,000 To Get Dillinger

Hitler Threatens Counter-Boycotts Of Other Nations

Gesture By Italy Disturbs Albania

Roosevelt Sets Up Board In Longshoremen Strike; Talks On Radio Tomorrow

Hitler Halts Move To Ban Stahlhelm; Papen Aide Seized

Hull Puts Blame For Debt Default On Nazis' Policies

Heat Of 97 Kills 3 Here; Throngs Sleep In Parks; Torrid Wave Grips Nation

JULY

Hitler Crushes Revolt By Nazi Radicals; Von Schleicher Is Slain, Roehm A Suicide; Loyal Forces Hold Berlin In An Iron Grip

Hitler Executes More Rebel Chiefs; Revolt Deaths Put As High As 200; Kaiser's Son And Papen Prisoners

Hitler Firing Squad Active All Day; Fate Of Hundreds Still Uncertain; Hindenburg Publicly Hails 'Victory'

Hitler Flies To Consult Hindenburg After Getting Papen's Resignation; Reich Facing Grave Economic Crisis

Resentment At Executions Spreads In Germany; Papen Keeps Nominal Post

2 Killed, 115 Are Injured In San Francisco Strike; Troops At Waterfront

Hitler To Reform The Storm Troops, Chief Peril To Him

Hitler Sets Truce For July In Reich, Leaves For A Rest

Hess Appeals To French To Keep Peace, But Dares Anyone To Attack Reich

Hitler's Storm Troops To Be Disarmed, Reduced From 2,500,000 To 800,000

Soviet Abolishes Its Secret Police

Johnson Offers One Code For All Minor Industries In NRA Clean-Up Program

Johnson Hits Nazi Killings; Says They Justify Fight For Free Press In America

Hitler Justifies Killings As 'Reich's Supreme Judge'; Defies Boycott By World

General Strike Tomorrow In San Francisco; Food Is Already Scarce, Services Stopped; Tie-Up May Extend To Portland And Seattle

Unions Will Ration San Francisco, Feeding City In Designated Cafes; General Strike On This Morning

Strike Paralyzes San Francisco Life, But Unions Allow Entry Of Food As Troops Help Police Keep Order

Strike Leaders Seek Arbitration, Asking That Roosevelt Intervene; San Francisco Vigilantes Raid Reds

Strike Now Collapsing In San Francisco Area; Shots Fired At Wagner

General Strike Called Off By San Francisco Unions; Troops Ready In Portland

50 Are Shot In Minneapolis As Police Fire On Strikers; Gas Routs Seattle Pickets

Ford Puts Trust In 'Pioneer Spirit' To Bring Recovery

Dillinger Slain In Chicago; Shot Dead By Federal Men In Front Of Movie Theater

Government Bent On Wiping Out Rest Of Dillinger Gang

Record Heat Grips West; Deaths To Date Put At 700; Chicago 105, St. Louis 110.2

Austrian Nazis Kill Dollfuss, Revolt Fails; 147 Plotters Held, Martial Law In Effect; Italian Army, Navy, Planes Ready To Act

Savage Fighting In South Austria; Starhemberg Orders Nazi Round-Up; Italy Holds 48,000 Men On Frontier

Austrian Nazis Routed In Provinces; Vienna Quiet, But Heavily Guarded; Italy Ready, Does Not Expect To Act

Austria Rebuffs Germany By Inaction On Von Papen; Duce Reported Urging Her

Shuschnigg Head Of Vienna Cabinet, Foe Of The Nazis

Yugoslavia Cautions Italy On Intervention In Austria; 'British Frontier' On Rhine

AUGUST

Hindenburg Is Gravely Ill, Hitler Summons Cabinet; Dollfuss Slayers Hanged

Von Hindenburg Dies At 86 After A Day Unconscious; Hitler Takes Presidency

Hitler Takes Presidential Power, Ending Title; Army Swears Fealty; Ratifying Election Set For Aug. 19

Manchester Bars Sales To Germans

Hitler Is Pressed To Give Assurance He Is Not Radical

Hitler Bars War; Asserts That 1918 'Was Lesson To Us'

65 Miles Of Torches Light Route Of Von Hindenburg To Tomb At Tannenberg

Roosevelt Visibly Moved In Tour Of Drought Area, Pledges Government Aid

Mrs. Antonio To Die In Chair Tonight

Roosevelt Nationalizes All Silver At A Price Of 50.01 Cents An Ounce; Promises Nation Broader New Deal

Estimate Of Grain Crop Is Lowest In 30 Years As Result Of Drought

Dr. Beebe Descends 2,510 Feet In Ocean

Nazi Bishop Defied Again By Pastors; Arrests Reported

Greater Drought Relief Is Studied By Roosevelt; Would Bar Profiteering

Kidnappers Seize Ontario Brewer, Demand $150,000

Roosevelt Takes Charge Of Drought Aid, Warning Food And Grain Gougers

1,200 In City Prison Rebel For 7 Hours

Hitler Declares Hand Was Forced By Hostile World

1% Tax On Gross Incomes, Some Mortgage Aid Voted As Legislature Adjourns

Hitler Endorsed By 9 To 1 In Poll On His Dictatorship, But Opposition Is Doubled

Hitler Aims To Win 10% Who Voted 'No' To The Nazi Cause

Gang Robs Armored Car In Brooklyn Of $427,000; Wide Hunt In 5 States

Capone In A Cell On Alcatraz Isle

Soviet Sharply Demands Japan Cease 'Aggression' And Free Seized Rail Men

Reciprocal Pact With Cuba Favors Island's Sugar, Rum And Many Of Our Products

Dorothy Thompson Expelled By Reich For 'Slur' On Hitler

Hitler Opens Saar Drive, Urging France To Expect German Victory In Vote

Strikers Eligible For Aid, Federal Relief Heads Rule; City Business Tax Delayed

Treasury To Use Profit Of $2,800,000,000 On Gold In Balancing The Budget

Time To Use Profit On Gold Indefinite, Says The President

Reich Can't Pay Any Debts For Years, Says Schacht; He Demands Cut In Total

SEPTEMBER

Textile Strike Is Extended To Wool, Worsted Trades; 650,000 Now Are Affected

Textile Peace Effort Fails; Silk Workers Ordered Out; New Ruling On Bargaining

Richberg Predicts 5,000,000 Families Will Be On Relief

Southern Textile Tie-Up Is Put At 50% By Unions; Profit Held New Deal Aim

Textile Tie-Up Short Of 50%; Unions Strive For Recruits; Some Violence Is Reported

Roosevelt Names Board Of Three To Mediate In The Textile Strike; Two Dead, 24 Shot In Riots At Mills

Reich Is Revealed Building U-Boats In Foreign Plants

Coolidge Aides Divulged Our Gun Designs To Help Produce Foreign Orders

Morro Castle Burns Off Asbury Park; 200 To 250 Are Listed As Dead Or Missing

182 Dead Or Missing In Morro Castle Fire; 375 Survivors Listed, 94 Bodies Recovered; Officers Will Testify At Inquiry Here Today

Morro Castle Fire Was Incendiary, Ship Officer Testify At Inquiry; Line Puts Dead At 87, Missing At 50

Chief Engineer Quit Ship, Did Not Go To Fire Post; Conboy Holds Crew Here

Radio Chief Lays Delay In SOS Call To Captain; Reveals Strife On Voyage

Rhode Island Legislators Balk Move For U.S. Troops; Governor Sees Red Revolt

City Halts All Cash Relief After The Aldermen Reject LaGuardia's Business Tax

All Needy Will Be Fed, Mayor Promises City; Federal Funds Cut Off

Textile Mills In South Plan To Reopen Today Under Guard Of Troops

Endeavour Wins First Race, A Test Of Men And Yachts; Fleet Acclaims The Victor

Lottery And Relief Taxes Voted By City Assembly; May Yield Only $15,000,000

Mayor Coll To Lottery As Opposition Mounts; Public Hearing Granted

Lindbergh Ransom Receiver Seized; $12,750 Found At His East Bronx Home; The Mystery Solved, Police Declare

New Jersey Prepares Murder Charge Against Hauptmann In Kidnapping; Linked To Lindbergh Ransom Notes

Lindbergh Returning Home To Aid Hauptmann Inquiry; Woman Accomplice Hunted

Grand Jury Inquiry Opens In Hauptmann Case Today; Lindberghs Flying Home

Col. Lindbergh Saw Aide Of Man Who Got Ransom; Handkerchief Sole Clue

Hauptmann Admits Noting Condon Phone And Address; Lindbergh Testifies Today

Hauptmann Is Indicted As Lindbergh Testifies; More Ransom Cash Found

Hauptmann Bail $100,000; Col. Lindbergh, Disguised, Sees Suspect Questioned

Blade Made By Hauptmann Found Hidden In His Cell; Insanity Plea Is Forecast

Trade And Income Taxes Made Law By LaGuardia; Other Levies Are Likely

OCTOBER

President Asks An Industrial Truce To Give NRA Labor Plans Fair Trial; A.F. Of L. Wants NRA Strengthened

City Plans 1% Income Tax, Also Levies On Estates And Mortgage Interest

Navy Men To Guard Liners On Voyages

Detective Bureau To Be Reorganized

End Of Boycott And Price-Fixing Considered By NRA

85 Slain In Spanish Strike; Radicals Cripple Country; Catalans Seek Secession

Catalonia State Secedes, Resisting Spanish Troops; Fierce Battle In Madrid

Revolt Is Crushed In Spain; 500 Dead; Barcelona Yields

Col. Lindbergh Identifies Hauptmann By His Voice; Murder Indictment Voted

Yugoslav King And Barthou Assassinated By Croatian As Ruler Lands In Marseilles; Europe Shocked, Fears Grave Complications

Aides Of King's Murderer Sought Through Europe; Sad Boy Ruler Starts Home

Inadequate Guard For King Stirs New Crisis In France; Yugoslavs Attack Italians

Companions Of Assassin Linked To King's Death; French See Wider Plots

Reich Denounces U.S. Trade Treaty; Asks A New Pact

1,156 Stay In Mine In Suicidal Strike

Hauptmann On The Stand Shouts Denial Of Murder; He And Wife Offer Alibi

Mrs. Stoll Is Found Alive; Insane Kidnapper Named; His Wife Got The Ransom

Hunt For Stoll Kidnapper Pressed, High Bail For Wife; Victim Bound When Captive

Brain Electricity Heard By Surgeons

Hauptmann Taken To Jail In Jersey; Appeal Rejected

Episcopal Bishops Favor Information On Birth Control

Scott And Black Leading By 8 Hours At Singapore; Dutch Fliers 2D, Turner 3D

Pretty Boy Floyd Slain As He Flees By Federal Men

Dutch Fliers And Turner Finish Second And Third In Air Raice To Melbourne

Bankers Greet Roosevelt With Ovation As He Offers Cooperation For Recovery

'Jafsie' Reported To Have Identified Hauptmann In Cell

Japan Takes Firm Stand For Naval Equality Now; 1935 Parley Is Imperiled

Roosevelt Action On Lynching Asked

Siam Hopes King Will Keep Throne

PWA Asks $12,000,000,000 For 5-Year Works Outlay; $5,000,000,000 For Housing

'Hunger Marchers' Routed At Albany; Rioting In Denver

NOVEMBER

Richberg Put Over Cabinet In New Emergency Council; Roosevelt
To End Pay Cuts

12,000 Put In Exile As Soviet Enemies

Roosevelt Backs Lehman, Evasive About Copeland; Moses Broadens
Attacks

Big Crowds Cheer Lehman And Moses At Rallies Closing Their
Campaigns; Chiefs Of Both Parties Confident

Australian Fliers Reach California From Hawaii, Finishing Pacific
Flight

3 Die, 27 Wounded As Bullets Sweep Political Parade

New Deal Scores Nation-Wide Victory; Lehman Wins, Legislature
Democratic; Taylor Victor, Reed And Sinclair Lose

New Deal Victory In Nation Grows; Republicans Win 3
Governorships; Redistricting First New York Aim

Flandin Forms Ministry As Doumergue Steps Out; Paris Quiet
Under Guard

Terrorism In Saar Shown By League

City Borrows $1,000,000 To Avert Relief Crisis; Plans New Taxes In Week

Betty Gow Coming To Face Hauptmann

Foreign Exchange Curbs, Excepting Those On Gold, Are Lifted By Treasury

City College Ousts 21 Student Rioters

Roosevelt Bars Plans Now For Broad Social Program; Seeks Job Insurance Only

Capital Business Parley Today Expected To Speed Support Of The New Deal

Income Tax Like State's Now Is Planned By City; Whole Program Fought

Italy And Austria Seek Reich Pledge

President Sees The Nation Developing All Its Power After Model Of Tennessee

Japan Asks Ratio Of 5-4-4 On Navies, Favoring Britain

U.S. Proposes Arms Pact For Control Of Traffic By A World Commission

Light From Brain Glows In Darkness

Record Arms Fund Approved In Tokyo

U.S. And Britain In Accord As Navy Talks Reach Crisis; Japan To Denounce Treaty

U.S. Note Protests Reich's Treatment Of Creditors Here

Nazis Secretly Cut Storm Troops; Transfers Swell the Reich Army

City To Vote 2% Sales Tax; Rise In Utility Levy Likely; Program To Net $58,000,000

Aldermen Vote New Taxes, 2% On Sales, 3% On Utilities, And Levy On Inheritances

Outlaw Nelson Found Dead From Slain Officers' Shots; Dutch Schultz Surrenders

Bolivian Army Reported In Flight On All Fronts; May End Long Chaco War

DECEMBER

Laval Bids Hitler To Show By Acts He Favors Peace

Borah Asks Republicans To Reorganize The Party To Give Liberals Control

Socialist Leaders Sanction Lining Up With Communists

France And Reich Agree On A Saar Payment Plan; Pact Protects Minorities

Pacific Fliers Missing After SOS Near Hawaii; Wide Search For Them

Code System Will Stay, Richberg Tells Industry; Admits NRA Fell Short

Davis Says Japan Upsets Security Of All In Pacific; Fears Costly Naval Race

Big Powers Halt War Talk In Yugoslav-Hungary Row; Tense Situation On Border

Nation-Wide Raids Jail 560 In Federal Narcotics Drive; 15 Arrested In New York

Yugoslavs Disturb League By Threat Of Lone Action, But They Cease Expulsions

President Demands Drive By All Forces Of Nation To Solve Crime
Problem

14 Dead, 40 Hurt, 50 Missing In Lansing, Mich., Hotel Fire; Many
Legislators Victims

Roosevelt Will Ask Laws To Take Profit Out Of War; Baruch To
Offer Program

Borah And Nye Demand End Of 'Big Business' Tie In Republican
'New Deal'

Job Insurance By States, With A Federal Subsidy, Roosevelt
Council's Plan

Russian Arrests Spreading Terror

Six Changes In NIRA Sought To 'Achieve' Labor Benefits; Ickes
Moves To End 'Waste'

Federal Board Rebuffs Utility Request To Join Test Of Validity Of
TVA

Roosevelt Confers Today On New York Utility Rates; $82,000,000
Write-Up Bared

Court House Fired As Troops Kill 2 In Lynching Mob

Zinovieff and Kameneff Seized In Soviet Killing, London Hears

Army Sees A Peril In Nationalizing Munitions Plants

Red Troops Cross Manchurian Line And Are Encircled

Christmas Spirit Enlivens The City; Aid For Destitute

President Calls On Nation To Show Courage And Unity; City Has
A Gay Christmas

15 Dead, 40 Hurt In Wreck; Crack Limited And Extra Collide At
Hamilton, Ont.

Plot To Kill Stalin With Foreign Help Linked to Assassin

16 Killed In Blast On Workers' Train

Einstein Offers New View Of Mass-Energy Theorem

Japan Denounces Treaty; Hull Reaffirms Our Policy; Britain And
U.S. In Accord

Rescuers Near 4 Fliers On Adirondack Mountain; Food Dropped
By Planes

1935: NEW YORK TIMES (365)

JANUARY

City Greets The New Year In One Of The Gayest Moods; Festive Places Crowded

Japanese Is Seized In Florida As Spy

10 Hauptmann Case Jurors, 4 Women, Quickly Chosen; Col. Lindbergh A Spectator

Col. And Mrs. Lindbergh On The Stand; Mother Identifies Baby's Garments; Father Says He Heard Ladder Crash

Col. Lindbergh Names Hauptmann As Kidnapper And Taker Of Ransom; Cool In 3-Hour Cross-Examination

Condon To Say Hauptmann Is Man Who Got Ransom; Defense Will Name Four

Reich Army Is Supreme As Sole Military Force Under Pledge By Hitler

Miss Gow Firm In Her Story Of Night Of Kidnapping; Identifies Baby's Clothes

Hauptmann Near The Scene With Ladder, Says Witness; Linked To Ransom Note

Condon Names Hauptmann As 'John' Who Got Ransom; Parries Defense's Attack

Breckinridge Backs Condon Who Acted On His Orders But Opposed Ransom Deal

Expert Says Hauptmann Wrote All Ransom Notes; $14,600 In Bills Identified

Miss Earhart Flies Pacific From Hawaii In 18 1/4 Hours; Finds Oakland Despite Fog

Saar Plebiscite Orderly As 98% Cast Their Votes; Nazi Total Is Put At 80%

Saar Goes German By 90%; League Deliberates Today; Anti-Nazis Already Fleeing

Saar Nazis Hail Victory As Foes Go Into Hiding; League Decision Today

Break At San Quentin Ends In Recapture, Warden Dying; 2 Bremer Kidnappers Slain

'You Stop Lying,' Hauptmann Rages At Federal Agent

Woman Says Hauptmann Limped After Kidnapping; 'You're Lying,' Wife Cries

Nazis Open Drive to Regain Memel; They Report Lithuania Mobilizing

Lindbergh Ready To Testify Again To Clear Servants

Hauptmann Not At Work March 1, 1932, Books Show; 'Sudden Wealth' Traced

Ladder Put Into Evidence After 15-Day Struggle; 2 More Name Hauptmann

Expert Traces Tool Marks On Ladder To Hauptmann, Part Of Wood To His Attic

Hauptmann Takes Stand, Swears He Was At Home Night Ransom Was Paid

Admissions By Hauptmann Open Cross-Examination; Shaken By Bitter Attack

Huey Long Troops Force His Foes To Surrender; Martial Law Declared

Hauptmann Faces Crucial Test Today Of His Composure

Hauptmann Admits Lying And Says Wilentz Lies Too; Still Protests Innocence

Hauptmann's Own Letters Discredit Story On Fisch As Cross-Questioning Ends

Three Hauptmann Alibis Backed By Wife On Stand; Another Witness Wavers

FEBRUARY

Hauptmann Alibi Backed By Two More Witnesses; Clash On Writing Expert

Witness Says He Saw Fisch With Sharpe Girl And Baby; Expert Aids Hauptmann

Lindbergh To Take Stand In Rebuttal In Aid Of Servants

Reich Invited As An Equal To Negotiate Arms Pact; Berlin Cool To Proposal

6 Alibi Witnesses Fail To Appear For Defense; Friends Back Hauptmann

Cafe Man Swears Fisch Was At Bronx Cemetery; Five More Fail To Appear

Expert Found No Prints Of Hauptmann On Ladder; Developed 500, Police None

Lumber Man Denies Rail Is From Hauptmann Attic; Defense Will Rest Today

Fisch Took Home Only $500 Sister Swears In Rebuttal; Hauptmann Alibi Attacked

Mrs. Morrow Last Witness; Backs Alibi For Her Maid; Jury May Get Case Tuesday

Oldest Known City in The World Believed Found in Mesopotamia

Reilly Accuses Servants, Charges Police Frame-Up In His Final Plea To Jury

'No Mercy,' Wilentz Plea; Intruder Shouts At Court; Case Goes To Jury Today

Hauptmann Guilty, Sentenced To Death For The Murder Of The Lindbergh Baby

Lehman Budget Adopted; Next Year's Income Tax And Gasoline Tax Raised

Japan Would Make China Accept Loan To Dominate Trade

Mayor Plans To Operate Key Buildings In Strike; Tries To Avert Walkout

Service Strike Ordered In 1,000 Buildings Today; Police Leaves Cancelled

Court Backs Government On Gold; 5-4 For Bond Payment In New Dollar; Business Surges Forward, Stocks Rise

Roosevelt Studies Move To Protect Government Fully On Any Gold Suits

Roosevelt Asks Renewal Of The NRA For 2 Years; Bill Drawn To Plug Holes

Berlin American Church Closes; Curb on Funds Imperils 2 Others

Mrs. Roosevelt Is 'Perturbed' By Verdict in Hauptmann Case

Military Centres Rise Near Berlin In Strict Secrecy

Hitler Dares Hate Of Foes In Hailing Nazi Party's Birth

Nation's Business Best Since 1933, Led by Autos, Steels and Textiles

Morgan's 900 Miniatures To Be Auctioned in London

NRA Loses Twice In Courts; 7A Voided In Weirton Case; Soft Coal Code Also Upset

MARCH

Policy Ring 'Higher-Ups' Hunted As Mayor Orders Gambling And Vice Drive

Saar Gives Hitler Delirious Ovation As It Rejoins Reich

French Dismayed As Pound Tumbles; Talk Of Devaluing

Greek Revolt Spreads; Rebels Now Hold Crete; Reserves Are Mobilized

U.S. Court Rules Albany Violates Interstate Law In Control Of Bulk Milk

240 In Vice Squads Shifted To Spur Racket Campaign; Courts Aid, Set High Bail

13 Subpoenaed As Court Charges A New Vice Ring; Immunity Offer By Dodge

20 Policemen Face Inquiry In Search For Policy Leaders

Greek Fleet Goes To Battle Rebels; Big Losses In Army

Havana Swept By Gun Fire; State Of Siege Proclaimed, With General Call To Arms

Treasury Uses $642,000,000 Gold Profit To Retire All National Bank Notes; Calls In Bonds, Reducing Public Debt

Threats Sent To Jurors And Rackets Prosecutor; First Indictments Voted

French Bill Calls for Big Warships To Rival Vessels of Italy and Reich

3,000-Year-Old Archives Found; Data Confirm Biblical History

$34,000,000 Profit In Year By Phillips Utility Group, Mack Committee Is Told

U.S. Arrests 2,000 In Surprise Raids On Nation's Gangs

Germany Creates Army Of 500,000, Orders Conscription, Scraps Treaty; Entente Powers Confer On Action

500,000 See Hitler Review Military Parade In Berlin; Reich Arrests 700 Pastors

Britain Protests To Hitler; Will Send Simon To Confer; Washington Also May Act

Britain Lines Up 2 Powers Behind Program At Berlin; French Demand Firmness

Police End Harlem Riot; Mayor Starts Inquiry; Dodge Sees A Red Plot

Germany Rejects Protests Made By France And Italy; Seeks New Deal In Europe

Secrecy On 859 Pay Rises Is Laid To Relief Bureau; Graft Rife, Hodson Says

Senate Votes Work Relief, 68 To 16, With Amendment To Expand Silver Currency

Poland Rebukes Germany And Now Turns To France; Britain's Envoys In Berlin

Hitler Insists The Soviet Imperils Peace Of Europe; Asks Austrian Plebiscite

Berlin Parleys Fruitless; End In A Warning By Simon; Memel Case Enrages Reich

British See Crisis Nearer As Cabinet Hears Simon; Nazi Fury On Memel Rises

Russia Asks Cooperation To Avert The Peril Of War; Commons Questions Simon

Senate Gets New NRA Bill Rushed To Avert Strikes; Labor Clauses Stronger

Ethiopia Refuses To Deal With Italy

APRIL

Power Shortage Found in Nation; Board Warns of Wartime Peril

Pope Warns War Would Be Insanity; Appeals For Hope

House And Senate Clash On Drastic Bills To End All Profiteering In War

Austria To Increase Army; Plans Two-Year Service; Poland Bars Eastern Pact

Pretty Girl Mends Stocking Run To Show the Supreme Court How

5 Billion Relief Bill Voted; President Ready To Speed Record Peace-Time Outlay

La Guardia Is Reorganizing Control Of The City Relief; Czar To Supersede Hodson

Nazis Balked In Danzig, Falling Short Of 2/3 Vote; Poles Protest Terrorism

Adolf S. Ochs Dead at 77; Publisher of Times Since 1896

Franco-Russian Alliance Within League Reported; Britain To Avoid Pledges

Wilgus Is Heard On Relief; Roosevelt Sets November For Peak Of Huge Spending

British Stand By Entente As Powers Meet In Stresa; Want Move By The League

Reich To Give Peace Pledge But To Avoid Security Pact; Stresa Solutions Speeded

Danubian Parley In Rome Is Decided On At Stresa; Franco-Italian Deal Near

3 Powers Agree To Resist Future Treaty Violations; French Protest To League

Widespread Air Alliances Are Developing At Geneva As League Gets Arms Issue

Reich Sponsored By 3 Powers, As Germans Warn Smaller Countries

League Censures Germany, Moves To Apply Sanctions For Future War Threats

Reich Protests To Britain Over Geneva 'Betrayal'; London Will Ignore It

U.S. Sharply Protests to Germany Against Discrimination on Debts

7-Alarm Fire In Brooklyn Floods I.R.T. With Smoke, Fells Many In Manhattan

2,471 Die In Formosa Quake That Wrecks 6,671 Homes; Army Quickly Gives Relief

Huge Soviet Force Near Manchukuo

600 Die In Quakes In Northern Iran; 3 Towns Leveled

Berlin's Gains in Air Bring Rival Capitals in Easy Reach

Germany Begins a Drive To End Non-Nazi Press

15,000 Nazis Rally Against Churches And For Paganism

12 U-Boats Built And Germans Push Training Of Crews

President In Talk To Nation Promise To Expedite Relief; Emphasizes Social Security

British Reply To U-Boats Likely To Be New Arming; Nazis Reopen Kiel School

MAY

Robot Plane Sets Mark From Coast

NRA Extended 10 Months In Senate Committee Vote; Lynching Bill Is Dropped

M'Donald Pledges British Air Arming And 3-Power Unity

France And Soviet Agree On Quick Aid In Event Of Peril

400 Die In Floods At Bahia; Gunfire Stops Avalanche; Large Buildings Destroyed

Goering Permits Writer To Glimpse German Air Gains

Britain Acclaims Ruler In Pageant Unsurpassed In History of The Empire

Senate Passes Bonus Bill With Two Billion Inflation, But It Might Hold Veto

Miss Earhart Sets Mark In 2,100-Mile Air Dash From Mexico To Newark

46 Naval Planes Take Off On Hawaii-Midway Flight; Storm Is Reported At Goal

President Welcomes Byrd Home As Guns Boom Salute to Explorer

450 Planes Ready To 'Attack Hawaii'

2 Die In Navy War Game, One As Destroyers Crash, Other In Dive Of A Plane

Lawrence of Arabia Dying After Crash on Motor Cycle

Mussolini Warns Powers To Leave Ethiopia To Italy

Einstein Is Silent As He Gets Medal

Billion Allotted On Works; Roosevelt Backs NRA Plan For Two Years' Extension

U.S. To Own Reserve Stock And Control Bank Credit Is Morgenthau Proposal

Soviet's Big Plane Crashes, Wrecked By Stunting Craft; 49 Killed In Two Machines

Pope Bids British Rejoin Church; Canonizes Two English Saints

Roosevelt Sets $19 To $94 As Monthly Relief Wages; Divides Nation In 4 Groups

Hitler Pledges Respect For Versailles Borders; Suggests Limiting Arms

House Overrides Bonus Veto, 322-98, Despite Strong Speech By President; 1,500 Business Men Ask NRA Renewal

Senate Kills Cash Bonus, Sustaining Veto By 8 Votes, But Campaign Begins Anew

Italy Submits To League On Ethiopian Arbitration; Britain Sways Mussolini

Mussolini Warns Italians May Fight

Reich Developing Fast-Moving Army

All NRA Enforcement Is Ended By President As Supreme
Court Rules Act And Codes Void; Whole New Deal Program In
Confusion

President Will Appeal To Nation With A Formula To Salvage NRA;
Industries Act To Retain Codes

Roosevelt Firm For Law To Retain NRA Principles; Appeals For
Speed Pour In

Conflicting NRA Views Pressed On Roosevelt; Labor Reports Pay
Cuts

JUNE

20,000 Die In Indian Quake; Wide Area Is Devastated; 43 British
Airmen Victims

Washington Studies Plan For A Quick Amendment Of Federal
Constitution

Kidnap Suspects Elude Capture In Long Chase, Enter Oregon Bad
Lands

Normandie Hailed By Throngs Here; Sets New Records

Roosevelt Will Keep NRA, Stripped Of Basic Powers; Cash Bonus
Fight Dropped

Power Strike In Toledo Is Ended By Union Vote After Government
Plea

Baldwin To Be Premier In British Shuffle Today; Hoare For Foreign
Office

House Votes NIRA Extension Cutting Roosevelt Power; Transport
Control Pushed

Mussolini Defies Britain And Likens His Policy To Hers

China Is Removing Troops And Japan Delays Action; U.S.
Warships Go To Area

'Grass Roots' G.O.P. Pledge Defense Of States' Rights; New NRA Pushed In Senate

British Get Reich To Limit Its Navy In All Categories

China Ignores Ultimatum; Japanese Troops Massed; Occupation Today Feared

Roosevelt Insists Congress Enact His Reform Program; Final NRA Vote Due Today

Skeleton NRA Is Extended; New Move On Hours And Pay; President Pushes Jobs Aid

Italy to Seize All Silver Money For Use in Ethiopian Campaign

President Sets Up New NRA And Picks Staff To Run It; $300,000,000 White Collar Aid

Britain Consulting U.S. On North China Crisis; Japan Reduces Forces

347 Convicts Hold Kansas Prison Pit; 9 Guards In Peril

Roosevelt Asks Inheritance Taxes And Other Levies On Big Fortunes; House Passes Wagner Labor Bill

Democrats Will Not Push Roosevelt's Tax Program At This Congress Session

British Ask Soviet To Discuss Navies; Paris Cool To Eden

Eden Finds Paris Firmly Opposed To German Navy

Navy Pact Details Left In Abeyance Until Wide Parley

Roosevelt In Sudden Move Demands Immediate Action On Wealth-Sharing Taxes

New Tax Program Pressed Despite A Revolt In House; Yield Is Put At $340,000,000

Hasty Tax Action Dropped As President Denies Order To Pass Bill By Saturday

Lehman Calls 4 Lawyers To Parley As All Decline To Head Racket Inquiry

Roosevelt Refuses To Drop His Fight On Holding Units; City Power Plant Blocked

Hoover Not A Candidate For The 1936 Nomination, G.O.P. Senators Are Told

JULY

Nazi Prison Camps Soften Discipline

House Defeats Roosevelt, 216 To 146, On 'Death Sentence' In Utilities Bill; New Test In A Vote Of Record Today

House Orders Inquiry Into Lobbying By Friends And Foes Of Utilities Bill After Beating President Again 258-147

Blockade Of Italy Reported Studies By British Cabinet

Einstein in Vast New Theory Links Atom and Stars in Unified System

President Rejects Ethiopia's Appeal For Peace Effort

U.S. Advises Its Citizens To Begin Leaving Ethiopia; 125 There, 113 In Missions

Britain Expected To Drop Her Effort To Curb Italy; Rift With France Deepens

37 Dead In Up-State Floods, 7 Missing, Many Homeless; Damage Is Put At $10,000,000

Federal And State Help Rushed To Flood Victims; Death Toll Rises To 41

Italy Said To Ask Part Of Ethiopia As Price Of Peace

Hull Joins With Powers Combating War In Africa; Tells Italy Of Concern

Hull Backs Kellogg Pact As Basis Of Our Policy; Reminder To Italy Seen

Coup By Heimwehr Looms In Austria As Chancellor Is Injured In Auto Crash

Mussolini Faces Ruin If He Yields In Africa Dispute

Jews Are Beaten By Berlin Rioters; Cafes Are Raided

AAA Processing Tax Illegal, U.S. Appeals Court Decides; State Rights Held Violated

League Prepares To Meet This Month On Ethiopia; Emperor Suggests Deal

Reich Strikes At Catholics; Rules Attacks By Priests Are Assault On Nazi State

Anti-Semite Police Chief Named To 'Purge' Berlin Of Jews And Communists

Priests Who Assail Nazi 'Purge' Today Will Be Arrested

Catholic Priests Silent On Nazi-Church Dispute, Except In South Germany

British End Naval Quotas But Seek To Limit Fleets; Propose A Parley In 1942

Anti-Semites Firmly In the Saddle As Persecution Spreads in Reich

Nazis Threaten Foreign Reporters For 'Lies' On Anti-Semitic Drive

Mussolini Offers Conciliation Plan In Ethiopian Row

Reds Rip Flag Off Bremen, Throw It Into Hudson; 2,000 Battle
The Police

Berlin Holds La Guardia Has Broken Trade Treaty; Washington
Regrets Riot

Ethiopians Attack Italians In Darkness, Killing Forty; Emperor
Replies To League

Racket Inquiry On; Grand Jury Picked And Dewey Sworn

Nazis Widen Religious War; U.S. Regrets Persecutions; Berlin
Protests Riot Here

AUGUST

Democrats Move To Defy President On Charity Tax; He Assails 'Thrifty' Rich

'Death Sentence' Defeated Again, House Voting 210-155; Republicans Delay Tax Bill

Big Power Yield To Italy On Ethiopian Arbitration And Call New Conference

Japan To Protest New York Cartoon

Goebbels Warns Of Greater Drive On Foes Of Nazis

Nazi-Catholic War Openly Declared; Pope Sees Trouble

New Deal Foe Is Victor In Rhode Island Election; Roosevelt Tax Aims Given

Strike By Unions Is Begun In Fight On WPA Pay Here, Threatening Wide Tie-Up

5 Slain At Toulon, Disorders Spread In French Strikes

President Bars U.S. Relief To All Who Quit WPA Jobs; More Strike On City Works

Income Tax Exemptions Cut By Senate Committee; Surtax To Apply At $3,000

Hitler Says Reich Is Ready To Meet Any Outside Peril

Senators Retreat On Taxes; Cut In Exemptions Dropped; Yield Now Set At $250,000,000

Senators To Investigate House's Coup On Hopson; Refused To Tell Income

Senate-House Rift Grows As O'Connor Holds Hopson, Ignoring Contempt Order

Senate Passes Its Tax Bill; Bans New Federal Issues Of Tax-Exempt Securities

Will Rogers, Wiley Post Die In Airplane Crash In Alaska; Nation Shocked By Tragedy

Italy, In Parley, Demands Control Of All Ethiopia; War Believed Inevitable

Ethiopia Parley Collapses As Mussolini's Reply Is 'No' To Anglo-French Proposal

Italy Bars All Peace Talk; Britain Weighs Sanctions, Wants To Know Our Policy

Demand To Vote U.S. Neutrality Now Halts The Rush Of Bills In Congress; London Acts Tomorrow On Ethiopia

President Acts In Neutrality Issue As House Balks After Senate Votes; Britain Won't Act Without France

Roosevelt Agrees To Bar War Arms Sales To Feb. 29; British To Wait On League

House Votes Neutrality; British Move Plane Ship; To Act Firmly In Geneva

Britain Is Sending Warships To Suez; Neutrality Voted

U.S. Protests To The Soviet Over Reds' Activities Here; Warns Of The Consequences

74th Congress Adjourns After Roosevelt Warning; AAA To Lend 10c On Cotton

Soviet Rejects U.S. Protest; It Denies Any Responsibility For Action Of Comintern

Italy Warns Of Dangers If Sanctions Are Applied, But Reassures British

Young Queen Astrid Killed As King's Car Hits A Tree; Leopold Slightly Injured

German Flies Plane by Leg Power, Bringing Dream of Icarus Nearer

SEPTEMBER

Italy To Call 200,000 Men Making 1,000,000 Under Arms; Her Reply To Sanction Talk

Reich Bishops Tell Catholics To Obey 'God And Not Men'

Liner Dixie On Florida Reef; 260 Passengers Are In Peril As Hurricane Lashes Keys

Seas Prevent Rescue Of 351 On Dixie; Captain Radioes That All Is Well; 75 Veterans Reported Dead In Storm

Hurricane Toll Exceeds 200; 164 Taken From The Dixie When Gale Halts Rescues

Italian Envoy Walks Out As Ethiopian Makes Reply; Soviet Asks League To Act

League Names Conciliators, Italy Yielding To Pressure; British To Act For Security

Truce While League Talks Reported Pledged By Italy; Pope Sees Hope For Peace

Doctor Shoots Huey Long In Louisiana State Capitol; Bodyguards Kill Assailant

Senator Huey Long Dies Of Wounds After 30-Hour Futile Fight For Life; Troopers Guard Louisiana Capitol

Long To Get State Funeral; Gov. Allen To Run 'Machine'; Foes See Chance To Beat It

Britain Demands League Act 'Against Aggression' And Pledges Her Support

Hull Invokes Kellogg Pact In Plea For Ethiopian Peace; League Awaits Laval Stand

Laval Puts France Behind League; Unity With Britain Isolates Italy; Rome, Stunned, May Leave Geneva

Italy Bars Compromises; Seeks Anglo-French Rift; League Rushes New Plan

Reich Adopts Swastika As Nation's Official Flag; Hitler's Reply To 'Insult'

Britain Is Sounding Powers On Sanctions Against Italy; De Valera Pleads For Peace

Italians Give Ray Of Hope They Might Yet Negotiate On 'Reasonable' Conditions

League Peace Proposals Give Italy A Part In Development Of Ethiopia; Britain Dispatches More Warships

Rome Expects Mussolini To Reject League's Plan; Geneva Studies Next Step

Italy Wavering As France Warns Rome Against War; May Ask New Negotiations

Italy Leaves Door Open In Rejecting League Plan; Rome Looks For New Offer

Mussolini Might Now Take Mandate Under The League; London
Denies Any Threats

League Firm On Peace Plan As The Ethiopians Accept It; Rome
Cabinet Meets Today

League Council Tomorrow Takes Up Mussolini Reply; Rome
Hopeful, London Firm

Ethiopians Are Mobilizing In The Frontier Provinces; Fascist Rally
Likely Today

League Decides To Invoke Sanctions If Italy Resorts To War On
Ethiopia; Next Move Is Now Up To Mussolini

Roosevelt Pledges Navy To Maintain Treaty Ratio, Building If
Others Do So

Hurricane Wreaks Havoc In Its Passage Over Cuba; Sweeps East Of
Florida

Britain Promises To Resist Any Aggressor In Europe; Rome Now
Sees War Soon

OCTOBER

Italy Ready To Begin War In Africa When Mud Dries; 30,000 Troops On The Way

Britain Asks French Stand If Italy Attacks Her Navy; Thinks Ethiopian War Sure

Big Italian Force Invades Ethiopia; Mussolini Rallies 20,000,000 Fascisti; Roosevelt To Keep US 'Unentangled'

Italian Airplanes Bomb Adowa And Adigrat; 1,700 Casualties Include Women And Children; League Council Acts On Sanctions Tomorrow

Italians Press Advance On Adowa; Fighting Reported On Other Fronts; League Group Reports Against Italy

Adowa And Adigrat Still Hold Out After Three Days Of Fierce Fighting; League Acts On Aggressor Tomorrow

Adowa And Adigrat Fall To Italians; Other Armies Advance In Ethiopia; Roosevelt Limits Travel On Ships

League Council Finds Italy Guilty; Moves To Invoke Sanction At Once; Italians Fortify New-Won War Lines

Italian Column Closing In On Aksum; Mountains Near Adowa Are Shelled; League's Experts Work On Sanctions

Hauptmann Loses His Fight For Life In Appeals Court

51 League Nations Condemn Italy; Name Committee To Apply Sanctions; Action Worries The Italian People

League Puts Arms Embargo On Italy, While Lifting That Against Ethiopia; Rome Reports Thousands Desert Foe

Italians Decide To Hasten Advance In Hopes New Ethiopian Defections; League Drafts A Financial Embargo

Mussolini Annexes Adowa; Italians Advance In South; League To Bar Basic Goods

Aksum Yields To Italians Without Firing A Shot; League Cuts Off All Loans

Italians March On Makale; Planes Raiding All Fronts; League Tightens Embargo

Britain Refuses To Withdraw Fleet; Rome Sees Intent To Stop Mussolini And Increased Peril Of European War

Anglo-French Relations Strained As British Demand Flat Reply On Aid; London Resents Pro-Italian Trend

Powers Halt Mediterranean Crisis; Britain And Italy To Reduce Forces; France Pledges Naval Aid To British

50 Nations Vote Boycott Of All Italian Exports; Cut Off 'Key' Materials

Ethiopians Trap 500 Foes; Italians Push Air Attack; Britains Hastens Armament

Italians Advance In South; Britain Checks Arms Ships; League
Invokes Paris Pact

Peace Parley Is Expected As Hoare Tells Commons Sanctions Can
Be Avoided

Schultz Is Shot, One Aide Killed And 3 Wounded

Schultz Dies Of Wounds Without Naming Slayers; 3 Aides Dead,
One Dying

Baldwin Warns Sanctions May Mean Naval Blockade; Wants Our
Attitude First

U.S. Pledges Moral Effort To Aid The League On Peace; Italians
Press On Makale

France Accepts Sanctions; Geneva Expects Our Help; Italians
Advance In North

Italians Make Big Gains On 400 Mile Line In South; Drive In
North Delayed

Mayor Orders War To End Gang Power; Chiefs Are Hunted

Germans Protest Churchill Attack As Libeling Hitler

NOVEMBER

League Moves To Enforce Italian Boycott By Nov. 15; Anti-British Riots In Rome

$416,861,000 Net Price Set For Transit Lines In Pact; City And I.R.T. In Accord

Italians Begin New Drive In North Toward Makale; Sanctions Start Nov. 18

120,000 Italians Advance 25 Miles Toward Makale; No Resistance So Far

3 Dead, 64 Hurt In Miami As Hurricane Hits City; It Sweeps Out Into Gulf

Republicans Win Majority Of 14 In State Assembly; Geoghan Elected In Brooklyn; County Reform Voted; Foes Seek Rebuke For The President And The New Deal

Kentucky Democrats Win; Party's Lead Here 360,000, Despite Loss Of Assembly

Italians View Makale From Camp On Heights; Ready To Enter At Dawn

Italians Gain On 3 Fronts; Take Makale And Gorahai; New Drive Begun In North

Japanese Troops Invade Shanghai To Avenge Killing

Italians In 130-Mile Drive Approach Jijiga In South; Expect Long Delay In North

Army Men Rise 74,000 Feet On Flight In Stratosphere, They Land Gently On Farm

Ethiopians Report Victory In Fierce Battle In South With Many Of Foe Killed

Anti-British Riots Flare Up In Egypt; Two Dead, 88 Hurt

250,000 See Quezon Sworn As Philippines President; He Warns Foes Of State

Hull Warns War Traders They Violate Our Policy; British Curb Sanction Foes

Italy Sends Staff Chief To Speed War In Ethiopia; De Bono Is Called Home

Fierce Ende Gorge Battle Described By Eyewitness; Sanctions In Force Today

'Siege' Of Italy On; Anti-British Riot Balked By Troops

Ellsworth Off On Flight Over Antarctic Wastes To Byrd's Little America

Ethiopians Repel Foe At Sasa Baneh, Massacring Many

Ethiopia Waging Hopeless Fight, Foreign Observers Are Convinced

Government As A Creditor Puts Pressure On Shipping To Halt Our War Exports

Italy May Leave League If It Extends Sanctions; Ethiopians Seize Towns

2 Women Patients Die, 36 Saved In Fire at Sanitarium in Jersey

Martial Law For Brazil Is Proclaimed By Vargas; Rebels Lose Pernambuco

Washington Not To Relax Effort To Curb War Trade; Italian Protest Expected

Italy Orders Army Moves To Warn Europe Of War; Makale Retreat Reported

Reich Declares All Men 18 To 45 Army Reservists

France, Britain Warn Italy Of Unit In Facing Attack; Sanctions Session On Dec. 12

DECEMBER

Chinese In North Give Up, Concede Autonomy Plan; Will Detach 2 Provinces

Britain And France Draft A New Offer To Mussolini; Would Halt Oil Boycott

Ethiopians Report Somaliland Drive Has Carried To Sea

Evasion To Be Prosecuted, Hull Tells Arms Traders; Britain Stands By League

Anglo-French Peace Plan Proposed As Alternative To Sterner Curbs On Italy

U.S. And Britain Warn Japan On North China Activities; Hull Cites Treaty Rights

Italian Air Raid Wrecks Dessye Palace, Hospital; 32 Killed, 200 Wounded

Lindberghs Still Believe in Guilt Of Hauptmann as Child's Slayer

New Ethiopia Peace Terms Fixed By Hoare And Laval As Final Offer To Italians

U.S. Asks 20% Naval Cut As London Parley Opens; Britain And Japan Cool

British Accept Peace Plan With Slight Modifications; It Goes To Rome And Addis

Ethiopia To Reject Terms, Envoy Forecasts In Paris; Storm In Britain Over Plan

Eden Gets League Council To Act On Ethiopian terms; Oil Sanctions Are Shelved

Peace Plan Held Doomed As League Publishes Text; Eden Prepares To Fight It

Democrats Search Old Files to Show Hoover Has Shifted

Peace Plan Revolt Rises; Little Entente Will Join Scandinavia In Opposition

Republican Convention In Cleveland On June 9; Party Chiefs Confident

Italians Are Forced Back As Battle Opens In North; Laval Is Upheld On Terms

Hoare Resigns, His Peace Plan Dead; Eden Admits Its Defeat At Geneva; Mussolini Renews Defiant Attitude

Baldwin Sustained 397-165 After He Confesses 'Error;' League Drops Peace Plan

Britain Rushes Egyptian Forts To Bar an Invasion From Libya

I.C.C. To Reduce Rail Fares To 2 Cents A Mile Maximum With 3 Cents In Pullmans

Lindbergh Family Sails For England To Seek A Safe, Secluded Residence; Threats On Son's Life Force Decision

America Shocked By Exile Forced On The Lindberghs; England To Guard Arrival

President Urges Christmas Spirit Of Peace And Unity

Pro-Tokyo Official Slain In Shanghai; Japanese On Guard

Supremacy In Air Is Hitler Answer To British 'Feeler'

Laval Fall Today Expected As Deputies Cheer Demand To Back Britain And League

Ethiopian Armies Battle Italian Forces In North; Laval Upheld 296 To 276

Deals On Colonies May Give Germany Portuguese Lands

Mussolini Acts To Calm Home Unrest By Pleading Difficulties In Ethiopia

1936: NEW YORK TIMES (366)

JANUARY

Swedes Are Slain As Italians Bomb A Red Cross Unit

Lehman Asks State Action To Set Up Social Program By Increasing Liquor Tax

Congress To Meet At Noon; Roosevelt's Speech Tonight Stirs Bitter Partisanship

Roosevelt In Message Dares Critics To Seek Repeal Of New Deal Laws; Condemns War-Making Autocracies

Roosevelt's Attack Opens 1936 Campaign In Earnest; Europe Sees No Oil Boycott

World Jewry To Be Asked To Finance Great Exodus Of German Co-Religionists

Supreme Court Finds AAA Unconstitutional; 6 To 3 Verdict Dooms Other New Deal Laws; Roosevelt Studies Upset; More Taxes Needed

Farmers Called To Capital To Draft New Aid Program; Cotton Faces 'Worst Crisis'

Roosevelt Asks Aid Of All For 'Progress And Ideals'; New Farm Policy Drafted

Democrats Set Convention For June 23 In Philadelphia; $200,000 Bid Win In 'Auction'

House Passes Bonus, 356-59; Soil Conservation Is Basis Of New Farm-Aid Program

Hauptmann Loses Plea To Court For Clemency; Talk Of Seizing Condon

Early 'Little Rains' in Ethiopia Destroy Roads, Halting Italians

Lehman Asks No New Taxes, Retains Emergency Levies; Budget Put At $308,667,248

Hauptmann Loses Plea For Federal Court Writ; Hoffman Still Undecided

Lights Out, City Paralyzed For Hours North Of 59th St. By Power Plant Failure

Ellsworth And Aide Alive And Well In Little America, British Rescue Ship Radios

Ellsworth Tells The Story Of Flight Across Antarctic; Battled A Raging Blizzard

George V Grows Weaker, Heart Strain Increasing; Family At His Bedside

President Extols 'T.R.' As Defender Of Social Justice

King George V Dies Peacefully In Sleep; Prince Of Wales Becomes Edward VIII

Edward VIII Is Proclaimed, Receives Fealty Of Nation; George's Funeral Tuesday

Five Powers Join In Pact To Offer A United Front Should Italy
Attack One

Zero Cold Kills 3 Here; No Relief Till Tomorrow; 13-State Area
Suffering

House Swiftly Overrides Bonus Veto By Roosevelt; Senate To Act
On Monday

Makale Line Cut In Bitter Fighting, Ethiopia Asserts

Italians Push On In South; Foes Retreat 268 Miles; Fight Continues
In North

Bonus Bill Becomes Law; Repassed In Senate, 76-19; Payment Will
Be Speeded

George V Is Buried With Regal Pomp As Nation Grieves

'Grass Roots' Open War On New Deal; Boom Talmadge

Plan For Big Tax Program Discussed At White House To Offset
Budget Losses

FEBRUARY

Huey P. Long's Widow Is Named To Fill His Seat in the Senate

Inflationists Adopt Plan For Drive In Both Houses If Tax Is Asked For Bonus

Poland Boycotts Oil Embargo Talks At Geneva Today

Repeal Of Three Farm Acts Recommended By President; House Gets Revised Aid Bill

President Moves To Cancel Billion In Unused Credits; End Of 'Priming' Indicated

Olympics Begin Today in Germany; 80,000 to Witness Winter Sports

Hitler Opens the Winter Olympics; U.S. Defeats Germany in Hockey

Slug 'Mint' Raided; Ton of 'Coin' Found

Britain Is Doubling Her Defense Plans To Offset Germany

Germany Insists She Owns Colonies Lost In World War

4 Powers Fix Cruiser Limit At 8,000 Tons For 5 Years; Battleship Accord In View

Nazis Strike Blow At Catholic Youth; 150 Leaders Jailed

4 Killed, 38 Injured In Panic As Lexington Av. Cafe Burns; 8 Dead In Fire At Lakewood

6 Fire Deaths Laid To Lax Supervision And Diners' Panic

Japan Now Finds Soviet Hits Back In Border Clashes

Roosevelt Asks Parley On Pan-American Peace To Meet In Buenos Aires

80,000 Ethiopians Routed By Foe In 6-Day Battle; Italians Gain In North

Supreme Court, 8 To 1, Backs TVA On The Sale Of Power Produced From Wilson Dam

$338,600 Gold Cache Is Seized In Raid on Deposit Vaults Here

Hauptmann Is Resentenced to Die; Leibowitz Suddenly Quits the Case

Spain Threatened By Martial Law As Leftists Riot

London 'Tin King' Jailed For A Year

Foreign Propaganda Here Is Denounced By Borah; He Again Urges Isolation

3 Legislators Are Named By Lehman On The Radio As Blocking Crime Bills

Eden Wants Britain Strong To Prevent European War; Rome Hints Of Reich Deal

Militarists Attempt Coup In Japan; Two Cabinet Leaders
Assassinated; Emperor Calls In Osumi, A Liberal

Loyal Army And Fleet Control Tokyo With Rebels Treating For
Peace; 80 Reported Dead In Street Fighting

Rebels Hold Posts In Tokyo; More Troops Move To City; All Night
Talk On Cabinet

Tokyo Rebels Surrendering After Ruler Orders Force; Strict
Censorship Revived

MARCH

Okada Alive, Holds Post; Relative Slain Instead; Revolt Leader A
Suicide

Italians Shatter Armies Of North In Bitter Fight; See War's Climax
Past

Italy Gets Choice Of African Peace Or Oil Sanctions

Strike Parley Deadlocked With 1,300 Buildings Tied Up; 5,000 In
Wild Park Av. March

Strike Parley Is Futile; Less Violence On 4th Day; Dodge Calls
Union Chiefs

Building Strike Spreading; Owners Bar 'Closed Shop'; 35 Hotels
Now Threatened

Reichstag Meets Today To Hear Hitler Outline New Stand On
Locarno

Hitler Sends Troops Into Rhineland; Offers Paris 25-Year Non-
Aggression Pact; France Mans Her Forts, Britain Studies Move

League Acts Friday On Rhineland; France Moving To Combat
Hitler; Mussolini Reported Seeking Deal

Locarno Signatories To Act Today; Eden Would Try Hitler Peace
Plan; Paris Censor Covers Troop Moves

French Bar Deal With Reich; Transfer Talks To London To Put Issue Up To Baldwin

France Remains Adamant As Locarno Powers Meet; British Seek Compromise

4 Locarno Powers Condemn Reich For 'Clear Violation' Of Treaties; Hitler Refuses To Quit Rhineland

French And Belgians Offer To Moderate Rhine Stand For British Military Help

Reich Invited To Parley As Locarno Powers Press For Franco-British Pact

Hitler Accepts League Bid In Terms France Rejects; British Still Expect Deal

League Bars Hitler Terms But Grants Him Equality; He Is Expected To Accept

14-Foot Flood In Johnstown Paralyzes Business Area; Waters Sweep Cumberland

Floods Sweep 12 States, Maroon Thousands; Pittsburgh In Darkness, All Traffic Cut Off; New England Hard Hit; Johnstown Deserted

134 Dead, 200,000 Homeless In Floods; Wheeling Deluged, Washington Hit, Wide New England Area Is Cut Off

Flood Paralyzes Hartford; Wide Ruin In New England; Waters Elsewhere Recede

Cold And Blizzard Hamper Relief In The Flood Areas; Crest Has Passed Hartford

New England Floods Fall; Hartford Under Troop Rule; New York Buffeted By Gale

Mussolini Nationalizes Key Defense Industries, Holding War Is Certain

Hitler Rejects All Terms But Promises New Offer; League Ends London Talks

U.S. And Britain Exchange Pledges Of Naval Parity; Limitation Treaty Signed

Reich Won't Halt Arming On Rhine Pending Parleys

Hitler Ridicules Powers' Demands In Plea To Nation

Germans Ordered To The Polls Today To Vote For Hitler

Hitler Gets Biggest Vote; Many Blanks Counted In; 542,953 Are Invalidated

Hauptmann's Plea Fails; 'No Stay' Says Hoffman Of The Execution Tonight

APRIL

Hauptmann Gets A Stay For At Least 48 Hours At Grand Jury's Request

Execution Of Hauptmann Set For Tomorrow Night; Further Delay Possible

Jurors Drop Wendel Case; Hauptmann To Die Tonight Unless He Gets A New Stay

Hauptmann Put To Death For Killing Lindbergh Baby; Remains Silent To The End

Emperor's Army In Flight, Pursued By Italian Planes, After A Stubborn Battle

Planes Follow Up Routed Ethiopians; Italians Press On

350 Killed By Tornadoes Over Wide Area In South; Property Damage Heavy

Italy Gives Pledge She Will Not Bomb Ethiopian Capital

Commission To Rule Europe Urged In French Peace Plan; 25-Year Status Quo Asked

Italy Admits Plan For Puppet State In Occupied Area

One Killed, 4 Hurt By Mailed Bombs At Wilkes-Barre

Troops Save Negro From Georgia Mob

League Of Nations In Americas Urged By 3 Latin States

Britain To Eschew Armed Sanctions Against Italians

$50,000,000 Art on Ship Aground Near Gibraltar En Route to China

Italians Occupy Dessye; Go 120 Miles In Five Days; Trade Cut By Sanctions

Italy Defiant On Terms, Tries To Bar The League; Drives On To Addis Ababa

League Peace Efforts Fail; Britain, France Avert Break By Deferring Oil Sanctions

Ethiopia's Peril Now Grave, Writer Finds At The Front; Emperor Can Still Fight

One Dead, Two Left in Mine Have Only 10 Hours to Live

Two In Mine Near Rescue; Hears Picks Of Men Cutting Through Last Rock Wall

Slides Delay Mine Rescue; Workers, Weary, Press On

2 Men Rescued From Mine After 10-Day Entombment; Robertson Asks For Steak

Press Fight Urged To Keep Radio Free From Censorship

Detective Called By Druckman Jury, Commits Suicide

Roosevelt, Here, Defends Cost Of 'Rebuilding' Nation; Urges
Lehman Re-Election

New City Charter Offered; Council Of 39 Is Created To End
Board Of Aldermen

Goering Dictator Of Reich Finances To End Quarrels

Roper Says Government Will Support Business If It Cooperates On
Jobs

$803,000,000 Tax Bill Wins By Vote Of 267-93 In House; Business
Attacks New Deal

MAY

Senators Move To Increase Tax Bill Yield $190,000,000 After Plea By Morgenthau

Force 40 Times That of Electricity Is Discovered in Hearts of Atoms

Emperor In Flight, Capital Looted, Ethiopia's Resistance Collapses; Foreigners Guarded In Legations

Shooting Mobs Ravage Addis Ababa; American Woman Among Many Slain; Britain Turning Away From League

Italians Reported At Addis Ababa; Legations Beat Off Many Attacks; Hull Directs Ours Be Abandoned

'Ethiopia Is Italian,' Says Mussolini As His Troops Occupy Addis Ababa; Quick Action To Protect Legations

Eden Asks League Reform; Italy To Annex Ethiopia; Bars Protests Or Parleys

Annexation Of Ethiopia Planned For Tomorrow; Italy Runs French Road

Dirigible Reaches New York At 4:55 A.M. In Record Flight; Goes On To Lakehurst Base

Italy Annexes Ethiopia; King Becomes Emperor And Badoglio Viceroy

Population Of U.S.A. 127,521,000 Last July 1, Up 3.9% in 5 Years

Robinson Taken By G-Men; Admits Stoll Kidnapping; Public Enemy Slate Clean

Revised Tax Plan Offered With Roosevelt's Approval; Inflation Fought In House

Frazier-Lemke Bill Beaten In The House By 235 To 142 After Warning On Inflation

Baldwin Seeks Reforms In League To Bring US In, With Germany And Japan

Rise In Income Tax To 5%, 18% Rate On Corporations, Now Favored By Senators

30 Hurt In Clash Of Seamen Pickets And Police At Pier

Germany Exudes Air Of Well-Being

High Court Voids Guffey Coal Law As A Violation Of States' Rights; Resettlement Loses A Test Case

Broader Powers Sought By Drukman Grand Jury In Appeal To Gov. Lehman

Lehman Not To Run Again; Blow To Party In State; Jackson Likely Candidate

18% Corporate Income Tax And 7% On Undivided Profit Agreed On By Senate Group

Axes Smash Clubs In Kansas Dry Raid

Many Deaths Laid To 'Black Legion'; Klan Link Charged

Officers of Black Legion Hunted By the Police in Michigan Deaths

Black Legion Men Held Without Bail On Murder Charge

Reich Puts 276 Monks on Trial, Accusing Them of Immorality

Senate Bill Gives Roosevelt Sole Control Of All Relief; New Snarl Over Tax Plans

Washington To Get Black Legion Data

Seamen End Strike, Fearing Cause Lost

Thousands Parade In City As America Honors Dead; Roosevelt At Arlington

JUNE

15 Escape as TWA Airliner Plunges Into a Chicago Lot

Supreme Court, 5-4, Voids State Minimum Wage Law; Another Blow, Says A.F. of L.

Canton Demands War on Japan; Seeks to Rally Whole of China

Parker Sr. Is Arrested In Wendel Kidnapping; Will Fight Extradition

France Crippled By Wider Strikes; Blum Is In Power

Landon Continues To Gain, May Dictate Platform; Borah Won't Support Him

'Stop Landon' Groups Fail To Unite, Awaiting Expected Attack By Borah; Vandenberg Rejects Second Place

Vandenberg And Borah Begin Drives To Stem The Rising Tide For Landon; Liberal Platform Demand Grows

Landon Sweep Is Checked By New York Group After Borah Blocks Combination Against Him; New Yorkers Bar Mills From Platform Post

Keynoter Denounces Roosevelt Policies, Demanding Tax Cuts And Balanced Budget; Landon Men Take Control Of Convention

Hoover Excoriates New Deal As Fascism, Demanding A 'Holy Crusade For Freedom'; Currency Plank Pledges Stabilization

Republicans Name Landon Unanimously; He Accepts Platform, Adding Own Ideas

Knox Nominated For Vice President, Hamilton Chairman, Convention Ends; Landon Prepares Vigorous Campaign

Japanese Land In Fukien As Canton Demands War; Two U.S. Ships Sent South

Barring of 3 Philadelphia Pastors Brings Walkout by Presbyterians

Inventor Is Slain Near Jersey Home; Footprint A Clue

Moore Murder Key Is Seen By Police In Jersey Suicide

Reich Has Air and Sea Strategy To Make A Blockade Impossible

Eden Smashes Sanctions; Says Alternative Is War; Firm On Mediterranean

4 Workers Killed, 12 Hurt In Crash Of Bronx Building

Congress Ends Its Session, New Tax Measure Enacted; Filibuster Kills Coal Bill

Smith Heads Group Calling On Democrats To Repudiate Roosevelt And The New Deal; Progressives Find Wagner Platform Weak

Loyalty To President Intensified By Revolts, Giving Him Complete Control In Convention; Move To Draft Lehman To Hold New York

Farley And Barkley Win Ovations For Roosevelt; Platform To Reassert Farm And Trade Policies; Lehman Expected To Run On Social Security Issue

Robinson Rallies Democrats With Defense Of New Deal; Committee Considers Platform Supplied By President; Roosevelt Expected To Draft Lehman After Convention

Democrats Adopt Platform Continuing New Deal; Favor Constitutional Amendments, If Necessary; Convention Abrogates Century-Old Two-Thirds Rule

Roosevelt Nominated By Acclamation; Demonstrations For Him And Lehman

Roosevelt To War On 'Economic Royalists'; Hailed by Throngs In Acceptance Ceremony; Garner Named As Weary Convention Closes

Steel Chiefs Defy Union; Pledge Resources To Bar Closed Shop In Industry

Bond Gang, Directed From Prison, Trapped Here In 'Perfect Crime'

JULY

Lehman Yields To Pressure, Will Run For Third Term; Roosevelt Hails Decision

League Is Leaving Ethiopia To Fate; Split On Reforms

Pope Orders World Drive To Raise Film Standards; Urges Boycott Pledges

Clashes In League Hold Up Disposal Of Ethiopia Issue

Nazi Mocks League In Danzig Hearing

Danzig Rift Turns Poles From Reich; League Test Seen

Lewis Opens Union Fight To Organize Steel Men; Ready For Long Warfare

Relief To 134,000 Families Planned For Drought Area; Roosevelt To Visit Region

Heat Kills 120 In Nation, Increases Crop Losses; No Real Relief In Sight

Heat Records Shattered With 102.3 Degrees Here; Nation's Death Toll 245

30 Die Here In 100 Heat, No Early Relief In Forecast; Western Crops Cut 40%

Rain Fails To End Heat Here After 72 Die In Four Days; Relief Forecast In West

Austria Pledged Hitler In Secret To Build Up Army

Break In Heat Wave Is Seen; Tugwell Go To Dakotas To Start Vast Relief Move

Rain And Cool Weather Move Slowly Eastward; Heat Deaths Near 3,000

United States Olympic Team Sails For Games Amid Rousing Send-Off

Edward Escapes Assassin As Policemen Block Aim Of Man At London Parade

Cantonese Leader Flees From China; Rising Collapses

Spain Checks Army Rising As Morocco Forces Rebel; 2 Cities In Africa Bombed

Rebels Gain In South Spain; Civil War Rages In Cities; Two Madrid Cabinets Fall

Revolt In Madrid Crushed; Fighting In Other Cities; Armed Masses Aid Cabinet

Rebels Win In North Spain And March Toward Madrid Where Red Rule Impends

Rebel Successes Reported In Spain; Checked In Madrid Drive, However; Consuls Tell Of Americans In Peril

Landon Pledges Strict Economy But Full Relief To Those In Need; Great Throng At His Notification

Landon Gets Wide Praise; Buffalo Speech In August To Open His Drive In East

Rebels Lose Fight In South Halt Their Push On Madrid; Retain 28 Of 50 Provinces

Queen Mary Sets Record For the Atlantic Crossing

Soviet Will Cut Imports to Add Gold Reserves for War Defense

Spain Orders Churches Confiscated; Control Of All Industry Is Decreed; Rebels Advance Steadily On Capital

Spanish Armies On Move For Six Major Battles; Madrid Sees Long Siege

Rebels Rush Men To Front For New Drive On Madrid; 2,000 Foes Slain In Ambush

AUGUST

France Asks 3-Power Conference For Neutrality In Spanish Crisis; Rebels Advance In Drive On Madrid

Spanish Rebels Now Drive to Capture Ports In North; Madrid Campaign Is Held Up

Threee Cities In Spain Fired By Intense Left Bombings; Rebels Advance On Madrid

Reich Warship Blocks Fire Of Spanish Ships At Ceuta; Reported Landing Sailors

U.S. Captures 4 Events; Owens Sets Jump Record

Owens Completes Triple As 5 Olympic Marks Fall

Germans Aroused By Left Shooting Of Four In Spain

Loyal Ships Fire Algecieras, Cut Off Foes In Morocco; Rebel Cruiser Ruins Gijon

Franco Promises A Liberal Regime, Favoring No Class

Loyalists Kill 800 Rebels In Battle Outside Madrid; Franco Forces Drive North

Corn Crop Worst Since '81; Relief on 'Disaster' Basis

32 German, Italian Planes Reach Rebel Army In Spain; Drive to Sea Begun In North

Rebel Defeats Reported In Drive To Sea In North; Air Raid On Madrid Near

Planes Bomb San Sebastian; Leftists Ready To Kill 700 If Warship Shells The City

U.S. Reduces Duties On Reich Imports

733 Executed In Madrid, 7,000 Others In City Seized; Rebels Near Port Of Irun

Rebels Slaughter Badajoz Leftists, Execute 1,200; Houses In Flames; Two Armies Drive On Reds In Malaga

Rebels Shell San Sebastian And Irun By Land And Sea; New Battle On Near Badajoz

Italy's Planes Ready To Help Rebels If France Continues Aid To Madrid; Capital Prepares For Early Attack

Increase In Drought Jobs Ordered By Roosevelt; He Will Ask More Funds

Reich Orders Its Warships Near Spain To Resist Force; Madrid Reports Victories

Rebels Losing In Battle At Cordoba, Prepare For Drive On Madrid Today; Germany Sends A Protest To Russia

Rebels Launch Drive, Attack Toledo, Fighting Within 40 Miles Of Madrid; Loyalists Meet The British Demands

Franco Stakes All In Drive To Take Madrid In 5 Days; Air Raid On City Reported

Germany And Russia Ban Arms Exports To Spain; Rebel Planes Bomb Irun

Roosevelt, If Re-Elected, May Call Kings, Dictators And Presidents To Great Power Peace Conference

Geoghan Blames Valentine For Drukman Case Fiasco; Lehman Joins In Questions

Geoghan Refused To Act In Murder, Valentine Swears

Hitler Suspends Trials Of Monks

Rebel Flier Bombs Heart Of Madrid; 17 Are Wounded

President Makes Protest To Both Sides In Spain Over Bombing Of Warship

SEPTEMBER

Machines Speeds Picking Of Cotton

$1,000,000,000 Rise In Deficit For 1937 Seen By Roosevelt; Relief May Cost $500,000,000

Fall Of Irun Is Imminent As Rebels Take Outposts; Diplomats To Seek Truce

Roosevelt Meets Landon In Cordial Drought Talk; Governor Offers His Plan

Anarchists Destroy Irun As City Falls To Rebels; Report Hostages Escaped

Fort Guadalupe Taken By The Spanish Rebels; Fuenterrabia Also Falls

Roosevelt Offers His Plan To Meet The Drought Crisis; For Jobs Rather Than Dole

Paris To Multiply Arms On Big Scale In Reply To Hitler

Reform Of The Government Is Planned By Roosevelt; Bureau Regrouping Studied

Hitler Disavows War Aim, Asserts Right To Colonies As Nazi Conclave Cheers

50,000 With Spades March For Hitler, Pledging Loyalty

Nuremberg Tense As 400 Planes Fly; Red Scare Grows

Landon In Final Maine Plea Scores Attempt to Control Business By The NRA And AAA

Hitler Warns Reds Millions Of Nazis Are Ready For War

Germans Planes Turn Tide To Rebels In Madrid Drive; Terror In Capital Revealed

Tammany Wins In City Poll; Brunner And Streit Victors; Couzens Behind In Michigan

Battle Rages At Maqueda, Southern Key To Madrid; TNT Laid To Raze Alcazar

Hurricane Batters Coasts Of Carolina And Virginia; Many Towns Are Evacuated

54 Lives Lost As Hurricane Sweeps Atlantic Seaboard; Gale And Rain Batter City

Hurricane Sweeps Out To Sea, Sparing New England Coast

Bomb Wrecks Newspaper And A Church In Havana; Four Killed, 27 Injured

Both Roosevelt And Landon Pledge New Aid To Farmers; Congress To Get Loan Plan

Landon Promises Farmers Cash Benefits To Equalize Aid of Tariff To Industry

Shanghai Area Occupied By Japanese Naval Force After Killing Of A Sailor

Rebels Storm Toledo Today; Flood Is Loosed Upon Them

French Cut Franc A Third On Monday; Gold Suspended; Parliament Called; Washington And London Cooperating

U.S. Backs Up Franc Deal, Buying Soviet Bank Pounds; Swiss, Dutch Will Devalue

Toledo Captured By Spanish Rebels; Alcazar Relieved

State Republicans Score New Deal; Opposition To Bleakley Crumbles; Democrats Center Fire On Landon

Roosevelt Hits 'False Issue' Of Communism; Repudiates Any Support By Its Advocates; Bleakley And Gov. Lehman Are Nominated

OCTOBER

Landon Based His Attack On Security Act On Report To Group
Backed By Filene

Ex-Gov. Smith Declares For Landon; Roosevelt Sees Budget
Balanced By Higher Revenue Without Tax Rise

Yanks Crush Giants, 18-4, A World Series Record; 45,000 See
Second Game

Foes Deadlocked In Hard Fighting

Paris Police Check Reds' Foes In Riots; 1,500 Seized In Day

Landon Advocates Anti-Lynching Law

Lehman Opens Campaign With Attack On Bleakley; Calls Program
'Supine'

Soviet Threatens To Help Madrid Unless 3 Powers Cease Aiding
The Rebels

Fair of 1939 Will Depict The 'World of Tomorrow'

Powers In Row Over Spain As Soviet Presses Charges; France Will
Not Aid Russia

New 4-Point Farm Program Is Outlined By Roosevelt; He Asks
Election Of Norris

Rebels Push Drive To Outflank Foe North Of Madrid

3 Powers Make Gold Deal; Exports To Central Banks To Stabilize Money Rates

Loyalists Battle Foe For Key Town; Rain Bogs Rebels

Roosevelt Says He Saved Business From Ruin And From Monopolies; Landon Sees Recovery Retarded

4 Union Leaders Accused In 'Riots'

Hoover Charges Faking In Accounts Conceals Huge Government Expense; Roosevelt Hits Out At Wall Street

Madrid Is Cut Off By Rail From Sea In Swift Advance

Rebels 18 Miles South Of Madrid; Capital Is Ready

President Quits Madrid; Rebels 16 Miles From City; Soviet Plans 'Drastic Step'

Landon Assails Roosevelt As Seeking 'Planned Society'; 50,000 At Los Angeles Rally

Roosevelt Likens His Tax Program To That For Which We Fought In '76; Landon Cheered By California Trip

Soviet Retreating On Threat To Help Leftist In Spain

Roosevelt Pledges Private Profit And Private Enterprise To Business; Landon Scores Attack On His Record

Soviet Accused By Britain Of Shipping Arms To Spain; Italy Also Called Violator

Germans Will Be Forced to Read Only Books by Hitlerite Authors

Landon Says 'Little Man' Must Pay New Deal Bills; President Talks To Negroes

Tammany Fights Charter And Proportional Voting; Landon Hits Farley 'Spoils'

City Throngs Cheer Roosevelt And Landon As They Open Final Battle For The East; Republican Candidate Greeted By Smith

Landon Challenges Roosevelt To State Aims On AAA, NRA, Unemployment, Relief And Budget; President Hits Drive To 'Sabotage' Security

Roosevelt Sets Security For All And End Of Inequalities As His Aim; Landon Campaigns In West Virginia

NOVEMBER

Roosevelt Defies 'Organized Money' Foes, Pledges Continued Fight For New Deal Aims; Landon, Closing, Promises Happier America

18 Vessels Tied Up Here; Strike Hits Other Ports; U.S. Ready To Intervene

Millions In Nation To Go To The Polls Today After Final Word By Roosevelt And Landon; Both Party Chairmen Confident Of Victory

Roosevelt Sweeps The Nation; His Electoral Vote Exceeds 500; Lehman Wins; Charter Adopted

Roosevelt's Plurality Is 11,000,000; Gains 14 Seats In House, 5 In Senate; Vote Here Held Blow To Tammany

Madrid Is Shelled As Rebels Push On Into The Suburbs

Government To Quit Madrid With City's Fall Imminent; Moors Drive Over Trenches

Battle In Madrid Suburbs; Cabinet Flees To Valencia; Tells Leftists To Fight On

Great Battle For Bridges Halts Rebel Madrid Drive; City Is Bombed And Shelled

Rebels Shift Their Attack, Threaten Madrid In North; Try To Cut Valencia Road

Roosevelt Repeats Pledge Not To Propose New Taxes; NRA Licensing Plan Studied

Leftists Recapture Town 4 Miles South Of Madrid; Capital Holds Foes At Bay

Madrid Drives Foe From Key Bridges; Insurgents Pause

Planes Fight Over Madrid; 4 Rebel Craft Fall In City; Loyalist Offensive Gains

Air Bombs Kill 53 At Defense Parley In Madrid Square

Rebels Reported In Madrid, With 3 Columns Advancing; Loyalists Say Drive Failed

Fires Dot Madrid As Bombs Kill 60; Foe Is In The City

Berlin And Tokyo Negotiating Pact To Combat Reds

Rome And Berlin Recognize Spanish Rebel Government; Leftists Open New Attack

Italy Ready To Give Franco Any Aid Needed For Victory; Guns, Planes Pound Madrid

Britain Avoids War Moves; Will Keep Aloof On Spain, But Would Defend France

Loyalists Hem In Rebels In Pitiless Madrid Fight; Icy Rain Checks Bombers

Fleet At Cartagena Raided By 'Foreign' Submarines, Madrid Communique Says

Britain Forbids Her Ships To Cary Arms To Spain; Refuses Right Of Search

Britain Sends Submarines To Patrol Spanish Waters As Franco Affronts Eden

Berlin-Tokyo Pact Signed; London, Paris Call It Blind To Conceal New Aggression

Soviet Dares Reich To Try Aggression; Says It Will Fail

Spain Appeals to League Against Reich And Italy; Council To Call Meeting

Litvinoff Sees Armed Bloc In Berlin-Tokyo-Rome Deal; Madrid Reports New Gains

Drive On Capital Of Rebels Made By Leftists In Spain; Russia Has 7,000 War Planes

DECEMBER

Reich Now Fears Japan Pact Imperils British Relations; New Battle Outside Madrid

Roosevelt Calls On The New World To Unite To Help The Old Avert War; For American Bloc Against Attacker

Edward May Abdicate Throne Today, Refusing To Break With Mrs. Simpson; Britain Is Astounded By The Crisis

Edward VIII Shows No Sign Of Yielding In Crisis; Sees Baldwin, Consults His Mother And York; Abdication Still Considered Likely Outcome

Cabinet Hears King's Answer To Baldwin At A Forty-Minute Early Morning Session; 60 M.P.'s Back Edward; Mrs. Simpson In France

King Held Certain To Quit Morrow; Churchill Asks 'Time And Patience'; Mrs. Simpson In Cannes; Yacht Ready

Cabinet Gives Edward VIII More Time; Aroused Public Opinion Forces Delay; Crowd Demonstrates In Downing St.

Edward VIII May Give Up Mrs. Simpson; She Makes Offer To End The Affair; King Is Still Undecided, Baldwin Says

King And Baldwin Hold 5-Hour Talk, But No Decision Is Yet Indicated; Doctor And Lawyer Fly To Cannes

British Ready For Abdication Today; Await Baldwin Common Statement; King Visits Mother In Secluded Lodge

Edward VIII Renounces British Crown; York Will Succeed Him As George VI; Parliament Is Speeding Abdication Act

Edward Sails From Portsmouth On Yacht After Broadcasting Farewell To Empire; Parliament Votes The Accession Of George VI

Chiang Kai-Shek Is Prisoner Of Mutinous Shensi Troops, Demanding War On Japan

Ex-King And 'Alien' Set Rebuked By Canterbury; Exile A Guest In Austria

Hitler Tells Nazis To Cease Attacks Upon Christianity

Chiang Lives, Says Nanking; Aide Is Seeking To Free Him; China Orders Martial Law

Young Roosevelt Saved By New Drug

Britain Will Keep Five Old Cruisers; War Danger Cited

Americas Promise United Opposition On Threat To Peace

Eden Urges Reich To Check The Flow Of Troops To Spain

Taxi Bandits Routed at Plaza; Auto Man Saves His Wife's Gems

Gomez Impeached, 111-45; Ouster In Cuba Held Sure As Senate Overrides Veto

Gomez To Defend Acts In Cuba Today At Trial In Senate

Reich Cautioned By Paris On Sending Men To Spain; Assurances
Are Reported

Nazis Face Choice On Spain As British Wean Italy Away

Gen. Chiang Freed; Arrives In Nanking; Ex-Captor On Way

Berlin Calls On Madrid To Release Seized Ship, Cargo And 3
Passengers; Paris Is Ready To Make Concessions

Pope Pius Suffers Increase In Pains; Doctors Stand By

Newark Dark For Hours As Fire Cuts Off Power; Business Is Shut
Down

Neutrality Law Revision Is Speeded By President To Halt Arms For
Spain

Pope Much Better After Long Sleep

1937: NEW YORK TIMES (365)

JANUARY

33,400 Men Are Made Idle; 'Sit-Down' Strikes Close 7 General Motor Plants

General Motors Faces Shutdown In All Plants; Union Bars Local Deals

Germans Stiffen Attitude On Spain; Fire On A Steamer

Britain And Italy, In Accord Hold Spain Must Be 'Intact'; Reich Would End Ship Clash

Reich Openly Mustering Its Public Against Spain; Rebels Gain Near Madrid

Federal Conciliator Tries To Arrange A Conference To Settle The Auto Strike

Roosevelt Calls On Courts To Help Adapt Constitution To Our Needs; Lehman Stresses Social Security

Reich, Italy To Halt War Aid Only If Others Leave Spain; British Fleet To Gibraltar

Paris Moves To Balk Reich As Troops Go Into Morocco; Army And Navy Made Ready

Rebels Close In On Madrid Under Heavy Gun Barrage; Say Defense Is Weakening

Britain Bars Volunteers To Spain; Calls On Other Nations To Do Same; Franco's Drive On Madrid Is Halted

24 Hurt In Flint Strike Riot; Police Battle Street Mobs; Governor Rushes To Scene

President Asks 105 Bureaus Be Put Into 12 Departments, Creating 2 Cabinet Posts

Auto Peace Talks To Be Held Today, But Clash Looms

Germany And Italy Decide To Back Final Franco Drive Before Armed Aid Is Halted

Court Picks Negro To Defend Green

$14,000 Gold Ingot Missing From Ship

Auto Strike Parley Off; Strikers Stay In Plants, So G.M.C. Bars Peace Talk

Rebels Close On Malaga After Hard 2-Day Battle; Il Duce Moves For Peace

Soviet Tries Radek And 16 On Saturday As Trotsky's Aides

Roosevelt Pledges Warfare Against Poverty, Broader Aid For 'Those Who Have Too Little'; Throngs See Inauguration In Pelting Rain

Auto Peace Talks Collapse; Sloan Quits As Lewis Calls On President To Back Union

150,000 Homeless In Floods; 16 Dead, Damage In Millions; Water To 72 Ft. At Cincinnati

Cold Grips Flooded Areas, Food And Shelter Scarce; 300,000 Flee
Rising Waters

Ohio River Flood Disaster Grows; Fire Adds To Peril In Cincinnati;
Roosevelt Directs Vast Relief Move

Whole Towns In Flight As Ohio Still Rises; Cincinnati Paralyzed,
Flood Nearing 80 Feet; Martial Law In Louisville As Chaos Spreads

Flood Crest Nears The Mississippi, With Levees Threatened In
Sweep; Mile Upon Mile In Wake Desolate

Flood Slowly Recedes On The Ohio, Leaving More Than 900,000
Homeless; Army Ready To Aid On The Mississippi

Tension Eases In Flood Zone With Levees Still Holding; Ohio
Valley's Danger Past

Mississippi Rises; Flood About Cairo At Critical Stage

Hitler Retracts 'War Guilt'; Demands Former Colonies; Says
'Surprises' Are Ended

FEBRUARY

13 Plotters' Pleas Futile In Moscow; All Will Be Shot

Troops Surround Plants Following Riots In Flint; Whole State Guard On Way

Court Orders Strikers Ousted Today; Men Wire Murphy They Won't Submit; Lewis Goes To Detroit To 'Face Crisis'

Auto Parleys Deadlocked; Talks To Be Resumed Today; Mobs In Flint Defy Sheriff

Auto Deadlock Unbroken But Murphy Reports Gain; Roosevelt Insists On Peace

Roosevelt Asks Power To Reform Courts, Increasing The Supreme Bench To 15 Justices; Congress Startled, But Expected To Approve

Court Reform Faces Fight, But Passage Is Forecast; Views Of Justices Sought

Roosevelt By Promise Of NRA And AAA Revival To Push Bench Reform

Compromise On High Court Sought By Some Leaders To Have 2 Justices Retire

Court Compromise Pressed As Opposition Increases; House Starts Action Today

1937: NEW YORK TIMES (365)

Auto Sit-Down Strike Ends; Agreement Will Be Signed At 11 A.M. To Quit Plants

Strikers Quit Auto Plants; Operations Resume Monday; $25,000,000 Rise In Wages

Roosevelt Seen Planning Public Appeal On Courts To End Congress Revolt

Glass, Wheeler Denounce Court Plan As La Follette Broadcasts In Its Defense

Cummings Scores 'Hysteria' On Roosevelt's Court Plan; Senate Revolt Is Spreading

Democrats Press Search For A Court Compromise; President Is Unyielding

Britain Announces A Record Program Of Naval Building

2 Amendments Proposed To Limit Court's Powers; A.F. Of L. Backs President

6 Dead, 10 Hurt In Explosion Aboard Battleship Wyoming; Shell Bursts In Gun Breech

Sandhogs' Leader In Strike Is Slain At Home In Jersey

Rosoff Seized As Witness In Strike Chief's Murder; Refuses To Go To Jersey

Roosevelt Aides Muster To Test Court Strength; Nye Denounces Program

Rollo Ogden Dead: Editor of The Times

Reich Business Fights 4-Year Plan; Will Present a Warning To Hitler

City Bar Assails Revision Of Court As 'Indefensible'

Borah Asks Amendment Giving States Control Of All Social Programs

Gas Barrage Ousts Fansteel Strikers In A Short Battle

Gas Bombs Injure 36 In Six Movies; Audiences Routed

MARCH

Pastor's Death in German Prison Causes Stir Among Protestants

High Court Backs Gold Ban; 5-To-4 Ruling Aids New Deal; Spirited Debate On Revision

Carnegie Steel Signs C.I.O. Contract For Pay Rise, 40-Hr. Week, Recognition; Deadlock On Naval Orders Broken

C.I.O. Drives On To Unionize The Entire Steel Industry; Independents Raise Wages

President Puts Court Plan On Basis Of Parity Loyalty; Says Problems Can't Wait

France Ends Curb On Gold To Regain Vast Sum Abroad

Foes Of Court Bill Reply To President, Assail 'Deception'

New Yorker Is Awed and Shocked In the Fog of a Dust Bowl Storm

Cruiser Sinks Spanish Ship That Outran U.S. Arms Ban; Passengers And Crew Safe

Roosevelt Asks That Nation Trust Him In Court Move; Resents 'Packing' Charges

Cummings Opens the Drive Before Senate Committee For Passage Of Court Plan

U.S. Takes Reich To Task Over Attacks In Press On La Guardia Incident

3 Senators Score Court Plan Here As Peril To Nation

Pittman Plans A Switch To 15 Permanent Judges, With Amendment Later

Hints Radio Chains Aid Court Change By Discrimination

Court Orders C.I.O. Strikers To Leave Chrysler Plants; Murphy Plans Enforcement

Detroit Strikers Defiant; City Faces General Tie-Up; Murphy Gets Hotel Accord

Murphy Warns Of Force As Strikers Defy Court Order At Detroit Plants; Sit-Ins Hotly Denounced In Senate

500 Pupils And Teachers Are Killed In Explosion Of Gas In Texas School; 100 Injured Taken From The Debris

School Deaths Under 500; Some Families Have Lost All Their Children In Blast

6,000 Chrysler Sit-Ins Defy Gov. Murphy To Use Troops; General Strike Threatened

7 Die In Puerto Rico Riot, 50 Injured As Police Fire On Fighting Nationalists

Hughes Against Court Plan; Wheeler Says It Originated With 'Young Men' Last Year

Chrysler And Lewis Meet Murphy In Lansing Today; 60,000 At Defiant Meeting

Lewis Agrees To Evacuate C.I.O. Sit-Ins From Chrysler Factories
By Morning; Workers Voting On Order Of Leaders

7 In Cafe Racket Guilty; Dewey Scores A Victory In Industrial
Gang War

Police Hero Named As Racketeers' Spy On Staff Of Dewey

Synagogue Swept By Fire In 82d St.; Incendiary Hunted

A.F.L. Brands Sit-In Strike Illegal Property Seizure; Chrysler
Deadlock Holds

Minimum Wage Law Constitutional; Supreme Court Switch Due
To Roberts; Glass Excoriates Roosevelt's Plan

Robinson Says Bitterness Drove Glass Into 'Error'; Lehman Plans
Wage Talks

APRIL

Paris Ready To Ask Step To Withdraw Aliens In Civil War

Move To Condemn 'Sit-Ins' Starts Sharp Senate Clash; New Michigan Strike Wave

House Moves For Sit-Down Inquiry Over Opposition Of Administration; C.I.O. Starts Purge Of Red Membership

15 Fast Russian Planes Cause Havoc In Cordoba; Swoop Low In Brief Raid

Dog's Police Stunt Kills Patrolman

Senate, 48-36, Blocks Move To Declare Sit-Ins Illegal; Guffey Coal Bill Passed

Chrysler Strike Is Settled; 65,000 Will Return To Work; New Parleys Over Details

Farmers Oust 500 Sit-Ins In Battle At Hershey Plant; Henry Ford Bars All Unions

House Bars Sit-In Inquiry, 236-149, In Stormy Session; Ontario Clamps Ban On C.I.O.

Ontario Expects Showdown Today On Openings G.M. Plant; A.F.L Union Adopts C.I.O. Plan

Premier Bars 'C.I.O. Agitator,' Breaking Up Oshawa Parley; Union Opens Campaign Here

Shots From C.I.O. Office Wound 9 of Rival Union

Supreme Court Upholds Wagner Labor Law; Hailed by Friends And Foes Of Bench Change; Unions See Sweeping Progress Within A Year

Roosevelt Still Presses His Bill To Change Court; May Take A Compromise

Taxis Slash Rates a Third; Operators Defy Police Ban

C.I.O. To Leave Strike In Oshawa To Local Unions; All I.M.M. Ships Face Tie-Up

Katonah Bandits Caught By Sheriff In Nebraska After Kansas Gun Fight

7th Suspect Taken Here In Gang Raid On Katonah Bank

Roosevelt Message To Ask $250,000,000 Cut In Expenses; Balanced Budget Now In '39

27 Nations Start Spanish Patrols; Valencia Defiant

Roosevelt Asks Economy; Spurs Congress To Action; Taxes Deferred Until 1938

Italy Held Unprepared to Protect Austria Against a German Coup

Mussolini Blocks Vienna Monarchy; Bans Military Aid

50 Hurt In Strike Battle At Stockton, California; Hershey Outvotes C.I.O.

Hirsch, In Nazi Jail, Resigned To Death

Vast German Fair Is Built In Secret To Rival Paris Fete

Herndon Set Free By Supreme Court

15% Cut In Appropriations Proposed As Session Goal; Roosevelt Reported For It

Reich Priest Gets 11 Years In Prison

Nazi Regime To Try 1,000 Monks In War Against Cathholics

MAY

Rebel Battleship Is Sunk By Spain's Loyalist Fliers; Cruiser Also Put To Flight

Hitler Defies Church Foes; Warns He Will Fix Morals; Soviet Shows Army Power

6,000 Called Out In 11 Film Crafts; Actors Hesitant

Pulitzer Prize for Novel Won by 'Gone With Wind"

Anarchists In Open Revolt Against Barcelona Regime; Italy And Reich Shape Bloc

Barcelona Quells Anarchist Revolt; Cabinet Is Altered

Hindenburg Burns In Lakehurst Crash; 21 Known Dead, 12 Missing; 64 Escape

Washington Starts Airship Inquiry; Death Toll Reaches 33; Lehmann Dies; Germany Will Continue Air Service

U.S. Navy Names Own Board To Investigate Airship Fire; 2 More Die; 30 In Hospitals

Coronation Week Opens As Rain Drenches Crowd; Notables Throng London

Gay London Is Prepared To Crown King Tomorrow; He Dines 400 Notables

Million Line Royal Route In Morning Mist As Procession Starts For King's Coronation; World Notables Gathered In Westminster

George VI And Elizabeth Crowned In Abbey; Millions Of Their Subjects Acclaim Them; King, On Air, Pledges Service To The Empire

Aid Of Queen Mary For Royal Wedding Sought By Windsor

Roosevelt, Back, Demands Passage Of His Court Plan And $1,500,000,000 Relief Fund

Foes Of Court Bill Insist Roosevelt Aids Their Cause

Communists Block Cabinet For Spain And Premier Quits

15 Democratic Senators Now Demand Showdown With Roosevelt On Court

Van Devanter, 78, Retires; Adverse Court Bill Report Voted By Committee, 10 To 8

J. Henry Roraback Kills Self By Shot

French and German Historians Agree to Purge Texts of 'Poison'

Basic 40-Hour Work Week, 40 Cts. Hour Minimum Pay, Planned In Federal Bill

Eckener Lays Airship Fire To Static and Leaking Gas

John D. Rockefeller Dies At 97 In His Florida Home; Funeral To Be Held Here

Supreme Court Backs Security Act On Job Insurance, 5-4, Pensions, 7-2; Roosevelt Asks A Wage-Hour Law

Italian Jews Told To Uphold Fascism Or Leave Country

Ford Men Beat And Rout Lewis Union Organizers; 80,000 Out In Steel Strike

I.R.T. Signs Pact With C.I.O.; 14,000 Get 10 P.C. Pay Rise; Davey Acts For Steel Peace

26 Hurt In Chicago Riot As Police Fight Strikers Marching On Steel Plant

Reich Battleship Set Afire By Spanish Loyalist Bombs; Italians To Fire On Planes

4 Killed, 84 Hurt As Strikers Fight Police In Chicago

JUNE

German Warships Shell Almeria, Killing 20, In Revenge For Bombing; Berlin, Rome Quit Neutral Patrol

Italian Warships To Halt Vessels Carrying Arms For The Loyalists; Hull Appeals To Reich And Spain

British Push Safe Zone Idea As Tension On Spain Wanes; Reich War Minister In Rome

Roosevelt Now Considering Compromise On Court Bill; For Action At This Session

Early Action On Court Bill Now Expected In Congress; President Criticizes Bench

W.J. Henderson, 81, Killed By Bullet

Catholic And Nazi Youth Clash In Munich, 10 Held; Hitler Warns The Church

C.I.O. Seizes Michigan Capital To Protest Pickets' Arrest; Snarls Traffic, Shuts Mills

Monroe, Mich., Calls Citizens To Arms To Guard Men Returning To Steel Jobs; Fights In Ohio As Pickets Are Disarmed

C.I.O. Power Strike In Michigan Ends; Gov. Davey Calls Steel Peace Parley; Police Battle Rioters In Youngstown

Monroe Deputies Smash Picket Lines And Allow 500 Men To Return To Jobs; Youngstown Seeking Special Police

Monroe Asks Martial Law As C.I.O. Calls Rally There; Youngstown To Keep Order

Gov. Murphy Orders Troops To Protect Monroe Today; Cambria Mill Still Running

Lewis Calls Mine Strikes To Halt Steel Mills' Coal; Troops Keep Monroe Peace

Senate Report Rejects Court Plan As Needless And 'Dangerous' Proposal

Roosevelt Says The Steel Companies, Agreeing Orally, Should Sign Pacts; Davey Plan For Them To Do So Rejected

Johnstown Mayor Appeals To Roosevelt To Intervene; Ohio Plants Seek To Reopen

Roosevelt Names A Board To Seek Steel Strike Peace; Moves To Open Mills Go On

Back-To-Work Drive On In Strike Zone; Youngstown Plans To Reopen Its Mills; Republic Scores 'Status Quo' Anarchy

Earle Blockades Johnstown Plant; Steel Officials Ignore Closing Order; City Is Under Rule Of State Police

Catholic Schools Are Shut By The Nazis In All Bavaria; Thousands Of Children Out

Roosevelt Asks Steel Plants Not To Reopen; Gov. Davey Orders Troops To Keep Status Quo After Operators Quit Mediation Conference

Strike Mediators Hopeful As They See Rival Leaders; Quiet Day At Steel Mills

Reich And Italy Quit Patrol; Nazi Ships Mass Off Spain; Rome Sees Pledges Ended

Mediators Ask Face-To-Face Parley Of Steel Leaders And C.I.O. Officers, But Republic And Youngstown Refuse

Chamberlain Sees Danger Of War In Spanish Crisis; Urges Europe To Be Calm

Gov. Davey Says Miss Perkins Asked Steel Chiefs Be 'Held Till They Sign'; She Explains She Suggested Subpoena

German Veterans Cheer For George At Rally In Reich

Michigan Limits Picketing, Curbs Outside Agitators; New Roosevelt Policy Seen

Public Tired Of Both Sides In Strike, Roosevelt Feels; Blasts Shut Cambria Plant

JULY

Japanese And Russians Reported Massing On Amur After Soviet Ship Is Sunk

Soviet Urges Withdrawal Of Both Sides At Border; Issues Big Defense Loan

Miss Earhart Forced Down At Sea, Howland Isle Fears; Coast Guard Begins Search

Storm Turns Back Plane Sent To Find Miss Earhart; Several Radio Calls Heard

Earhart Heard By Honolulu; Definite Signals Reported From Flier By Coast Guard

Earhart Searchers Arrive At Point Reported Given By Plane On Radio; Transatlantic Fliers Reach Goals

Earhart Search Shifting To Southeast Of Howland After Fifth Fruitless Day

Warship's Planes Start Search For Miss Earhart; No Definite Signal Heard

Colorado's Planes Again Hunt In Vain For Miss Earhart

U.S. Agrees to Sell Gold to China In Move to Aid World Currencies

95.6 Heat Kills 25 More On 4th Torrid Day Here; Brief Respite Promised

Fifth Day of Heat Wave Kills 38 Before Thunderstorm Cools City

Fighting Continues In China; Big Japanese Force Moving; Tokyo Sends Stiff Demands

Revolt Against Court Bill Grows With House Joining; Copeland Chides Roosevelt

Senator Robinson Dies Suddenly; Senate Faces Fight On Leadership And Fate Of Court Bill Is Doubtful

Roosevelt Demands Fight For Court Change Continue; Says Nation Backs His Aims

Sharper Fight On Court Bill Follows President's Letter; He Is Neutral On Leadership

Revolt Within Tammany Imperils Copeland Race; Republicans Lean To Him

China's Chief In The North Makes Terms With Japan; Agrees To Withdraw Army

Lehman Calls Court Plan Dangerous And Asks Wagner To Vote Against It; Proponents, Resentful, Press Fight

Court Change To Be Shelved For Present, Capital Hears After White House Parleys; Roosevelt Sees Both Rivals For Leadership

Court Bill Drives Collapses; Foes To 'Write Own Ticket'; Barkley Made Leader, 38-37

Court Bill Is Killed, 70 To 20, As Senate Galleries Cheer; Lower Court Change Likely

City to Liberalize College System Under Fusion-Controlled Board

Wilson In A Rage Over Earle 'Spies'

Japanese Planes Bomb The Chinese In New Outbreak

Japanese Troops Cut Off In Peiping, Many Killed; Tokyo Plans Stern Action

Battle For Peiping Begins; Chinese Are Pushed Back; One Regiment Annihilated

Chinese Attack At Tientsin; Foreigners Seeking Safety; Peiping Defenses Bombed

Air Raid Spreads Ruin In Tientsin As Chinese Battle With Japanese; Garrison Is Trapped Near Peiping

Chinese Routed By Japanese In District 100 Miles Wide; Tientsin Uprising Crushed

AUGUST

Japanese Batter Tientsin As Chinese Still Hold Out; 'Puppet State' Is In Revolt

30 Soviet Churchmen Are Tried On Charges of Fascist Plotting

Sullivan Heads Tammany, Pledges Aid To Copeland; New Deals Foe In Saddle

Roosevelt Hints Justice Will Be Nominated Soon; Borah Sees No Vacancy

Whalen Drops Out Of Race; Mahoney Will Replace Him; Copeland To Continue Fight

Japan Threatens A Wider Conflict; Warns Foreigners

Senate Passes Housing Bill With $4,000 A Family Limit; New Court Bill Up Today

Senate In 59 Minutes Votes Changes In Lower Courts; Session End By Aug. 21 Seen

Japanese Occupy Peiping To Set Up Rule By Army; Nanking's Threat Defied

Japanese Navy Men Slain By Chinese Near Airfield; Shanghai Situation Tense

Maylor And Copeland File For Republican Primary; Rival
Democrats In Race

Revolt In Congress Blocks Chief Roosevelt Measures; Democrats
Lead Uprising

Senator Black Nominated As Supreme Court Justice; Quick
Confirmation Balked

Shanghai Battle Goes On As Rain Halts City Fires; Chinese Planes
Attack Ship

Chinese Air Bombs Kill 600 In Shanghai; 3 Americans Among The
Foreign Dead; Hull Sends Plea To China And Japan

Japanese Forces Attack Shanghai In Early Dawn By Land, Air And
Sea; U.S. Evacuating Women And Children

Shanghai Battle Rages During Night; Casualties Heavy; Troops
Pouring In; Thousands Of Foreigners Seek Safety

Black Confirmed By Senate, 63-16; Debate Is bitter

Roosevelt Assails Critics As Enemies Of Democracy; Stands By
Present System

Chinese Thrust Foes Back In Fierce Drive At Shanghai; U.S. Insists
River Stay Open

U.S. Flagship Hit, 1 Killed, 18 Injured; One-Fourth Of Shanghai Is
Burning; Chinese Take Offensive In The North

Japanese Air Bombs Spread Fire And Terror In Shanghai; Raid On
Nanking Is Repulsed

60,000 Troops Battling Near Peiping In Drive By Chinese To Regain North; 400 Killed In Shanghai Foreign Zone

Shanghai Bomb Dead 195, Wounded 475; Chinese Set Fires To Block Japanese; Hull Again Makes A Plea For Peace

Japanese Set Nankow Trap, But Are In Peril At Peiping; Firing At Shanghai Intense

Japanese Blockade Coast Of China To Foe's Shipping; Mass For Shanghai Push

Japanese Fliers Shoot British Envoy; London Is Considering Sharp Action; Tokyo May Search Foreign Vessels

Hull Warns Japan And China On U.S. Ships And Nationals; Britain Preparing Demands

Japanese Bombs Kill 200, Wound 400, In Sudden Plane Attack On Shanghai; China Offers To Take Hull Peace Plan

Sharp British Note Demands Redress For 'Inexcusable' Wounding Of Envoy; China And Russia Enter Anti-War Pact

U.S. Warns Ships To Avoid Shanghai After Chinese Bomb Big Dollar Liner; Warships Ready To Save Americans

SEPTEMBER

Japanese 'Big Push' Ready At Shanghai And In North; China
Apologizes To U.S.

Japanese Win Air Control, But Are Held Up On Land; Bitter Battle
At Woosung

Chinese Bombs Upset Japanese Plans To Land Troops And Guns
For Drive; Warships Will Escort Our Shipping

Chinese Put Troopships To Fight, Bar Japanese Landing At
Shanghai; Big Guns Pound Whole Enemy Line

Three Powers Ask End Of Warfare Around Foreign Areas At
Shanghai; U.S. Will Oppose Aggressive Nations

Japan Opens Big Offensive On Whole Shanghai Front; Chinese
Lines Hold Firmly

Russia Charges Italy Torpedoed Two Of Her Ships

Russia Wants Indictment Of Italy At Parley; Objects To Bid To
Reich; London And Paris To Act On 'Piracy'

Reich, Italy Reject 'Piracy' Parley; Britain, France Determined To
Act; U.S. Warns Ships In Mediterranean

'Piracy' Parley Opens Today; Britain Would Curb Soviet; Rome
And Berlin Stay Out

Nyon Powers Act To Suppress Piracy; To Patrol Mediterranean By Zones; Russia Threatened To Take Own Steps

Britain And France Get Patrol Duty With Way Open For Italy To Aid Them; Roosevelt Determined To Avoid War

Soviet 'Cleansing' Sweeps Through All Strata of Life

China Appeals To League, But Avoids Charge Of War; Army Retires At Shanghai

Rosevelt Named Black Unaware Of Link To Klan

British Insurers Now Put Curb On Trade To Orient; Japanese Gain In North

La Guardia And Mahoney Defeat Copeland In Heavy Primary Voting; Upsets In Tammany Leaderships

Roosevelt Renews His Fight For Whole Social Program; Challenges Foes On Court

British Destroyer Attacked By Plane Off Coast Of Spain

Colmery Warns Legion On Perils To Democracy; Convention Opens Today

Legion Urged To Help Avoid War; Warned On Nazi And Red Perils; World Mood Dangerous, Hull Says

2,000,000 In 5th Ave. Cheer Legion In Great Pageant; 85,000 In 18-Hour Parade

U.S. In Sharp Note To Japan 'Objects' To Nanking Raids; Fifty Planes Attack City

20 Chinese Cities Bombed; 2,000 Casualties In Canton; Japanese Halted At Paoting

Britain Expresses 'Horror' Of Bombings, Talks Boycott; Our Fleet To Stay In China

80 Japanese Planes Bomb Nanking For Seven Hours; 200 Killed; Heavy Damage

Russian Note Warns Japan To Spare Nanking Embassy; Protests Worry Japanese

Japanese Submarines Sink Fishing Junks; Hundreds Die; 22 Nations Condemn Raids

Soviet Envoy Flying Home From China, Aims Secret; Hull Backs League's Step

Black Hints He Won't Resign, Parries Questions On Klan; Now Drafting Radio Speech

OCTOBER

No Hint By Black Of Details Of Talk Over Radio Tonight

Black Admits He Joined The Klan; Quit, Then Ignored 'Unsolicited' Card; Cites Record As Liberal In Senate

Black's Senate Silence Still Puzzling Capital; His Seating Now Awaited

London Mob Raids Fascists' Meeting

Justice Black On Bench As High Court Receives Protests On Seating Him

Roosevelt Urges 'Concerted Action' For Peace And Arraigns Warmakers; League Committee Condemns Japan

U.S. Condemns Japan As Invader Of China; Drops Neutrality Policy To Back League; Geneva Calls Meeting Of 9-Power Nations

U.S. To Join 9-Power Parley, But Avoids Taking The Lead; Japan Will Stand By Policy

Chamberlain Pledges Cooperation To End Horror Of Two Major Wars; Japan Makes Reply To U.S. And League

Mussolini Rejects Parley On Volunteers In Spain; Britain To Keep Door Open

France Is Turning From Plans To Aid Spanish Loyalists

Black Suit Barred By Supreme Court; Labor Hearing Set

Roosevelt Calls Congress For Nov. 15 To Act On Pay, Hours And Crop Control; For 'Balanced Abundance' In Nation

British-French Ships Act To Bar Taking Of Minorca; Italian Parley Plan Wins

Rival Airplanes And Guns Bring Terror To Shanghai; Chamberlain Courts Italy

Roosevelt For Mediation To Stop Warfare In China; Eden Asks Italy To Recede

U.S. Joins Far East Parley But Retains Independence; Davis Is Our Soul Delegate

Chinese Air Fleet Bombs Foes' Ships In Six Large Raids

Airliner Crashes On Utah Mountain; 19 Believed Dead

Landon Asks Republicans To Cut Roosevelt Power; Objects To One-Man Rule

Italy And Germany Agree To 'Token' Withdrawals; Commission To Go To Spain

Danzig Nazis Link Free City To Reich; End Center Party

Hitler Receives Windsors Simply

Both Sides Claim Gains At Shanghai In 4-Day Battle

Tokyo Flier Raids Riders; Briton Dies; Americans In Peril

Reich to Rally World's Germans In Support of the Four-Year Plan

Japanese Capture Chapei; Area A Mass Of Flames; Chinese Ranks Mowed Down

Strong Chinese Line Halts Foes' Big Push At Shanghai; U.S. Guns To Fire On Planes

18,000 Cheer Mayor In Plea To Retain Honest City Rule; Mahoney Presses Red Issue

Japanese Shell Foreigners In Shanghai, Killing Britons; Threaten To Widen Attack

Rival City Tickets Predict Victory; La Guardia Aide Sees 750,000 Majority, While Mahoney Forces Expect 350,000

NOVEMBER

Mayor Expected To Sweep His City Ticket Into Office; Borough
Results In Doubt

Record Mayoralty Vote Today Likely; Thugs Rounded Up; Police
At All Polls; Candidates Campaign To The Very End

La Guardia Is Re-Elected By 454, 425; Dewey, M'Goldrick And
Morris Win; Fusion Controls The Board Of Estimate

Brussels Parley Develops Move To Align Democracies In Resistance
To Dictators

Hitler To Mediate In Far East War; Both Sides Accept; Armistice
Likely; Brussels Powers To Question Tokyo

Hitler Mediation In China Now Held To Be Premature

Italy Joins Japan And Reich In Pact Against Communism; New
World Line-Up Is Seen

Flow Of Gold Now Away From U.S.A.; Credit Base Firm

Chinese Quit Shanghai Area, Burn Buildings In Retreat; Rome Pact
Arrouses Soviet

Japanese Bombing Nantao To Rout Trapped Chinese; Many
Civilians Are Slain

Brazil A Corporate State; Vargas Takes Full Power; Washington Is Concerned

Chinese End Fight In Shanghai Area; Harried In Retreat

Stronger Front To Japan Sought In Brussels Parley; British Seek Reich's Amity

Mild Criticism Of Japan Is Drafted By 19 Powers; Action Is Left To Future

Congress Convenes Today With Its Course Uncertain; Revolt On Taxes Possible

Congress Puts Business Aid To Fore After Roosevelt Asks Tax Revision; No Specific Program Yet In Sight

Congress Program Snarled, With Filibuster In Senate And Disorder In The House

Move To Repeal Profit Tax Makes Headway In Senate; Roosevelt Program Lags

Grim Throngs Quit Nanking As Troops Move To The Front

Chautemps Victor As Chamber Hears Of Hooded Menace

Business Aid To Be Enlisted By President For Housing; Soft Coal Prices To Be Set

Senate Farm Group Drafts Bill For Five-Crop Control; Defies Roosevelt On Cost

Roosevelt Moves To Limit Congress To His Program; Leaders Pledge Tax Delay

Business Pressed To Aid Recovery; House Committee Acts On Tax Relief; SEC Again Warns Stock Exchanges

Edison Groups Plan Outlay Of $112,000,000 In Two Years After Talk With Roosevelt

Franco Hastening Plans For Attack

Roosevelt For Tax Revision 'When Congress Is Ready'; Prepares Housing Message

300 Henchmen Of Marinelli Questioned By Grand Jury After Round-Up By Dewy

French In London Find British Favor Appeasing Of Reich

President Asks 16 Billions Be Spent In New Housing; Would Pare Building Costs

DECEMBER

Call For Cut In Road Funds Starts Revolt In Congress; Willkie's Utility Plan Told

Lehman Orders Marinelli To Answer After Dewey Files Three New Charges

House To Act On Wage Bill As It Is Forced To Floor; Its Fate Is Still In Doubt

U.S. Troops Halt Invasion Of Our Arena In Shanghai; Japanese Abandon Raid

$800,000,000 Budget Slash Reported On Capitol Hill; $500,000,000 Cut In Relief

Delbos Reassured Of Desire Of Poles To Resist Fascism

Japanese Reach Nanking; 90 Planes Bomb The City; Sun's Tomb Surrounded

Du Pont Sees 3,000,000 Jobs If 'Fog' On Taxation Is Lifted; Budget Shows Expense Rise

Industry Offers Recovery Program, Addressing Special Plea To Labor; Brookings Urges Profits Tax Repeal

Industry Invites New Deal To Join It In War On Slump; Hopkins Adds 350,000 To WPA

Roosevelt Road-Cut Plan Defied By House Chairman; President
Gives Rail Stand

Italy Leaves The League; Great Crowd Cheers Duce In Pledge To
Back Peace

U.S. Gunboat Sunk By Japanese Bombs; 1 Dead And 15 Hurt 18
Missing; British Warship Hit, Seaman Dead

U.S. Demands Full Satisfaction From Japan, With Guarantee
Against Further Attacks; Thought Ships Chinese, Admiral Explains

Hull Note Demands Formal Redress Ignoring Earlier Japanese
Apologies; New Peiping Regime To Rule Shanghai

Japanese Air Chief Ousted For Bombings On Yangtze; Tokyo To
Send U.S. New Note

Panay Attack Deliberate, Yarnell Report Indicates; Our Protests
Broadened

U.S. Naval Display Reported Likely Unless Japan Guarantees Our
Rights; Butchery Marked Capture Of Nanking

Hirohito Gets Panay Facts; He May Answer President; Note Will
Deny Ships Fired

Col. Hashimoto Ordered Panay Firing; Political Influence Bars
Punishment Of Leader In 1936 Army Coup In Tokyo

Tokyo Militarists Delay Guarantees Asked By U.S.; General
Defends Troops

Roosevelt Bars Peace At Any Price; Landon, Knox Pledge Unity In
Crisis; Japan Warned By British Premier

Japan Denies Army Fired Intentionally Upon Panay; British Alert
At Hong Kong

NLRB Finds Ford Guilty Of Violating Labor Law; He Plans Fight
In Courts

Japan In New Apology Says Guilty Have Been Punished;
Hangchow Reported Taken

America Accepts Japan's Apologies, But Insists On Future
Safeguards; Blockade Of Tsingtao Is Declared

Fall Of Tsinan Is Reported As Japanese Drives Go On; Hull Note
Relieves Tokyo

Scientists Called To Rally Humanity Against Warfare

Roosevelt For Larger Navy; Voices 'Growing Concern' As Trend Of
World Events

Razing Of Tsingtao Begun By Chinese; Reprisal Is Likely

Roosevelt Is Backing Drive For Cut In Monopoly Prices; Fight To
Finish, Says Ickes

1938: NEW YORK TIMES (365)

JANUARY

Roosevelt Cuts Silver To 64.64 Cents; Denies Drive On All Big Business; FTC Acts On Building Supply Costs

Roosevelt Drafts Program For New Session Tomorrow; Census Shows 7,822,912 Idle

Capital Eagerly Awaiting Roosevelt Message Today; Congress Convenes At Noon

Roosevelt Asks Capital And Labor To Cooperate In National Recovery; Denounces Abuses By Small Groups

Roosevelt Asks Business To Join Him In Controlling New Industrial Production

1 Billion Deficit In 7 Billion Budget; Defense Outlay Raised To $990,000,000; President Cites Slump, World Unrest

15,000 Cheer Hague For Ban On C.I.O.; 'Reds' Are Defied

Roosevelt Deal With South Wins Support Of Wage Bill; Rail Rate Basis Is Involved

Roosevelt Pledges Fight To Finish On 'Autocratic' Business Minority; Lehman Urges Party To Be Realistic

Japanese Leaders Fail To End Clash On Policy In China

Ludlow War Referendum Is Defeated In The House As Roosevelt Scores It

Industrialists See Basis For 'Better Understanding' After Talk With Roosevelt

President Asks 46 Leaders Of Business To Conference; 'Self-Policing' Plan Is Seen

Chautemps Cabinet Quits After 9 Socialists Resign; Fall Of Currency Is Issue

Roosevelt Insists On The Dissolution Of Holding Companies, Banks Included; Hears Plea For Recovery Policy Soon

Stanley Reed Goes To Supreme Court; Known As Liberal

6,000,000 Found Ill In Day By Survey Of National Health

Fixed Liquor Prices Ended Here by National Distillers

Earle Will Ask The Government To Take Over Anthracite Mines

Roosevelt Plans A Council To Help Formulate Policy Coordinating All Interests

King Farouk Makes Farida His Queen; Wild Fete In Cairo

Whole TVA Is Ruled Valid, Its Power Program Upheld; Auto Men Pledge Changes

Violent Magnetic Storm Disrupts Short-Wave Radio Communication

Chinese Reds Firm For A Revolution, Army Leader Says

SEC Bans Short Selling; Says 11 Exchange Men Led Shorts In Falling Market

Roosevelt Fights Pay Cuts; Holds Industry Must Lead The Way To Reduce Prices

Roosevelt Stand On Wages Brings New Congress Drive For Business Tax Relief

U.S. Protests Anew To Japan On More Outrages In China; Embassy Official Slapped

President Asks Battleships, Cruisers, More Army Funds, In Great Defense Program

600 Seized In Raids As Police Hit Back At Hold-Up Gangs

Anti-Lynching Bill To Give Way Today For Housing Action

FEBRUARY

Torpedo Sinks British Ship Off Spanish Coast, 11 Lost; Swedish Neutral A Victim

Britain Sends 8 Warships After 'Pirate' Submarine; Calls Powers To Confer

Dixie Davis Seized As Rackets Chief On A Tip To Dewey

'Small Business Men' Score New Deal And It Works; Ask Tax Relief And Economy

Hitler Assumes Control Of Army; Retires 15 Generals And Shifts 25; Ribbentrop Made Foreign Minister

U.S., Britain And France Will Call On Japan For Data On New Warships By Feb. 20; Want 35,000-Ton Treaty Limit To Stand

Japan May Reveal Navy Plans To U.S., But Not Under Pact

Niemoeller Trial Opens in Secret; He Clashes With Reich Attorney

Japanese Attack Shifted In North To Entrap 400,000

Anti-Jewish Edict Voided In Rumania

Patriarch Forms Cabinet As Anti-Semitic Regime Of Goga Falls In Rumania

Carol Gives Army Control In Nation; Press Is Censored

Japan Refuses To Reveal Naval Data; U.S. Expected To Exceed Treaty Limit; Britain Prepared For An Arms Race

Austro-Reich Pact Reported As Step To 4-Power Accord

Gold Sterilization Policy Eased To Cheapen Money And Add To Bank Funds

Austria Capitulates To Germany; Pro-Nazis Get Key Posts In Cabinet; Berlin Hails Unity Of Two Nations

Berlin Outlines Policy For Austria; Sees A Reorganized Central Europe; Gloom Pervades Vienna; Nazis Freed

Secret War Debt Parley Held In The White House; New Proposals Opposed

Hitler Expected To Decree Pan-Nazi 'Monroe Doctrine'; London-Rome Pact In View

Austrian Issues Split British Cabinet; Eden And 2 Others Threaten To Quit; Europe Tensely Awaits Hitler Speech

Hitler Demands Right Of Self-Determination For Germans In Austria And Czechoslovakia; Eden Resigns In Crisis Over Britain's Policy

Commons Backs Chamberlain Policy, As Eden Scores Yielding To Threats; New Talks With Italy Start Soon

Chamberlain Calls League Impotent; He Wins 330-168 Victory In Commons; French Decide To Speed Armaments

China Carries War To Japan As 12 Bombers Fly There; 3 Formosa Cities Are Raided

Free Austria Guaranteed, Schuschnigg Tells Diet; Hitler Ready To Quit Spain

Battleship Best Weapon For US, Roosevelt Insists; Sees Air Peril Overrated

Spy Ring In U.S. Army Bared; German Girl, Two Soldiers Seized As Foreign Agents

Spy Hunt Pressed By Agents On Trail Of Two More Here

MARCH

Hitler Again Orders Nazis Here To Quit Bund and All Such Groups

City Sets Record Tax Rate; House Bill Approved, 17-7; Lehman's Program Passed

26 Lives Are Lost As Throngs Flee California Flood

144 Dead Or Missing In Pacific Floods; 20,000 Homeless; Huge Property Loss; Los Angeles And Wide Area Isolated

82 Known Dead, 128 Missing In California Flood Debris; Wide Area Still Isolated

6,000 Taxi Drivers Locked Out; Row With Union Halts 50 Fleets

Rebel Cruiser Torpedoed In Spanish Naval Battle; British Rescue 400 Men

Chamberlain Wins Commons' Backing On Foreign Policy

Roosevelt Acts On TVA; Calls In Three Directors To Present Facts To Him

'Third Basket' Tax Defeated By Wide Margin In House; New Revenues Are Sought

Wide Disorders In Austria; Troops And Planes Moving; Reich Seen Directing Nazis

Nazis Seize Austria After Hitler Ultimatum; German Troops Invited To Maintain Order; Seyss-Inquart Chancellor; Powers Protest

Hitler Enters Austria In Triumphal Parade; Vienna Prepares For Union, Voids Treaty Ban; France Mans Border; Britain Studies Moves

Austria Absorbed Into German Reich; Hitler Commander Of United Armies; Miklas Ousted; Plebiscite On April 10

Hitler Enters A Cheering Vienna; No Force Can Part Us, He Responds; Britain Sets Up New War Service

Loyalist Spain Begs Help Of France, Admitting Situation Nears Collapse; Paris Sees New Nazi-Fascist Menace

France Wins British Pledge Of Mediterranean Navy Aid; Will Not Intervene In Spain

Polish Army Set To Invade Lithuania Unless Demands Are Accepted Today; 'Clericals' Are Arrested In Vienna

Poland Stands By Her Ultimatum; Lithuanian Cabinet For Acceptance; Powers Bring Pressure To Avert War

Lithuania And Poland Decide On Peace; Hitler Would End Czech-Soviet Pact; Hull Scores Austrian Coup, Accepts It

Times Bureau Aide Jailed In Moscow; Assisted At Trial

Morgan Defies Roosevelt; Refuses To Resign His Post Or To Retract TVA Charges

A.E. Morgan Dismissed From TVA By Roosevelt; H.A. Morgan
Now Heads It

Selfish Few Block Nation, Roosevelt Says In Georgia; Scores South's
Low Wages

British Would Aid France; Bar Czech Pledge, But Say They Might
Have To Fight

Roosevelt Holds Out Haven To Oppressed Of All Lands Within
Quota Provisions

Goering Is Acclaimed in Vienna; Warns Jews Must Quit Austria

Rebels Invade Catalonia In Day Of Smashing Drives; Rome Warns
Paris Of War

APRIL

Reorganization Bill Passed By The Senate, 49 To 42; New Deal Wins On Utilities

U.S. Protests To Mexico On Seizure Of Oil Plants; Britain Supporting Action

President Has No Inclination To Be A Dictator, He Asserts; 'Lacks The Qualifications'

Reorganization Wins Test In Turbulent House Session; Passage Tomorrow Sought

House Rebels At Speed On Reorganization Bill; Vote Off Till Next Week

Compromise Stems Revolt On The Reorganization Bill, But Legality Is Questioned

Insurgents Take Lerida; Nearing Tortosa In South; Madrid Heavily Shelled

$1,000,000 Racket In Taxicabs Bared As 5 Are Indicted

Mayor Ends Cut In Relief After Council Votes Taxes; New Levies Start Monday

Innitzer Retreats on Nazi Appeal After 2-Hour Talk With the Pope

Socialists In Riot At French Senate Over Blum Rebuff

House Kills Reorganization Bill, 204 To 196; Vote Called Lack Of Confidence In President; New Public Works Drive In Recovery Program

Senate Passes Its Tax Bill; Votes To Forbid Exemption Of Future Treasury Bonds

Hitler Is Backed By 99.08% Of Vote In Poll On Empire

Roosevelt Plans Appeal To Nation As Garner Balks At 'Pump-Priming'; Railroad Relief Put Up To Congress

New Deal Spending Decided In White House Conference; Split With Garner Denied

Senators Revolt As Roosevelt Acts To Save Surplus, Capital Gains Taxes; Recovery Program Also Faces Fight

Roosevelt Asks Expenditure Of $5,000,000,000; On Radio, He Urges 'United Nation Will'; Congress Expected To Accept His Program

Spanish Rebels Reach Sea, Cutting Loyalists In Two; Occupy 16 Miles Of Coast

Anglo-Italian Pact Signed In Rome; Italy To Quit Spain When War Ends; France Moves For Deal With Rome

Carnegie Relative Vanishes In Plane

Rebels In Tortosa; Retiring Loyalist Blast All Bridges

Moves To Check Spending Are Started In Congress; Glass Attacks Program

End Of Surplus Profits Tax To Relieve Unemployment Asked In Report To Senate

Organs Live Days In Lindbergh 'Pump'

Modified Surplus Tax For Two Years Retained In Senate-House Compromise; Senate Wins On Capital Gains Levies

Nazis to Purge Vienna Library; 'Non-Aryan' Works to Be Burned

Russia Rounds Up Religious People; Archbishop Held

Prague Rebuffs Henlein; Bars Pro-German Policy; Stands By Its Alliances

16 Business Leaders Offer Cooperation For Recovery; Roosevelt Sees Ford Today

Talk With Roosevelt Fails To Change Ford's Opposition To Government In Business

Britain And France Agree On A Defensive Alliance; Unified Commands In War

Roosevelt Asks Inquiry On Monopoly; Says Private Power Leads To Fascism; Rules Committee Blocks Wage Bill

MAY

NLRB Acts To Reopen Cases Of Ford And Republic Steel; Follows Rebuke To Wallace

500,000 Throng Fair At Music Festival; Many Turned Away

Commons Votes Rome Pact; Chamberlain Extols Duce As Hitler Starts For Italy

Mussolini Greets Hitler In A Resplendent Rome; 300,000 Applaud Visitor

Roosevelt Backs Lifting Arms Embargo On Spain; Congress Agrees It Fails

Italy's Navy Holds Review For Hitler, Biggest Since War

Wage Bill Forced To Floor By Petition In The House; Early Passage Is Doubtful

Invasion Of Jersey City Halts As Hague Crowds Gather To Bar Speeches

Italians Air Power Is Shown To Hitler In Rome Farewell

Ford Mexican Unit Closed By Strike; Labor Pact Asked

Sit-Down Strike Is Ruled Illegal; State's Power Upheld in Illinois

Brazil Crushes A Revolt; Vargas Family Fights Off Fascist Guards At Palace

Hughes Appeals To Lawyers To Seek Qualified Judges; Roosevelt Sees New Spirit

U.S. Drops Plan To Repeal Arms Embargo On Spain; Franco Forces Advance

Mussolini Says Fascists Will Fight Together To End If Democracies Make War

Gains By Japanese Admitted By China; Tactics To Change

Farley Creates A Furor In Pennsylvania Primary By Asking Vote Be Split

C.I.O. Beaten By Earle Ticket In Pennsylvania Primary; Pinchot Loses In 'Comeback'

Pennsylvania Results Blow To New Deal And Its Chiefs; Republicans See New Hope

Gerson Disclaims Part In Name Shift; Defends Marxism

Government Demands Court Rehear The Stockyard Case; Jackson Assails 'Reversal'

Czechs Put 400,000 Troops Near Borders Of The Reich; Two Sudeten Germans Slain

Firm Stand By The Czechs Eases Tension In Europe; Nazi Troops Withdrawing

Long Henlein-Hodza Talk Leads To Hope In Prague; Reich Troops Again Retire

Henlein Breaks Off Talks, Renewing Tension In Prague; New Troop Moves Reported

J.J. Hines Arrested By Dewey As Policy Racket 'Fixer'; Released In Bail Of $20,000

New Deal 'Purge' To Have Next Test In Iowa Primary

Roosevelt Scores Tax Bill, Asks Revamping Next Year; It Becomes Law Unsigned

Mandalay Sunk In Collision In Fog With Linder In Bay; 314 Rescued By The Acadia

Levine Boy's Bound Body Washed Ashore On Sound 94 Days After Abduction

Peace Is Pledged As Nations Honors Dead Of Six Wars

JUNE

Wallace Is Again Rebuked By Court In Stockyard Case; Labor Board Wins On Steel

Senators Allow Roosevelt $125,000,000 In Direct Relief; Resent Plea For Free Hand

Senate Refuses To Prohibit Use Of PWA Cash To Compete With Private Enterprises

Senate Votes Pump-Priming; Bars Earmarking Of Funds And Control By The States

Thomas Is Routed As Riot Halts Speech In Newark; 400 Police End Fighting

Canton Is Bombed For Seventh Time; 300 More Killed

Gillette Winning In Iowa Over Wearin In A Primary Testing New Deal 'Purge'

New Deal Presses 'Purge' Despite Defeat In Iowa; Roosevelt Backs Hopkins

Canton Is Ablaze Under New Raids; Casualties 8,000

Insurgents Bomb 3 Ships As London Studies Reprisals

Hague Testifies Red Pilots Forced Ban On C.I.O. Rallies; Denies Free Speech Is Issue

U.S. Acts To Check Sale To Japanese Of Our War Planes

Wage And Hour Bill Ready; Social Importance Hailed; Workers Can Go To Courts

Rail Legislation Dropped In Drive For Adjournment, Set For Tomorrow Night

Congress Passes Wage Bill, Drops Lewis's 'Blacklist'; Hopes To Adjourn Tonight

Fight On Flood Control Bill Upsets Adjournment Plan; Lewis Loses On 'Blacklist'

Congress Adjourns Sine Die; Members Off For Campaign; Session Spent $12,000,000,000

Lehman Warns U.S. On Wiretapping

Anti-Jewish Drive Covers All Reich; Arrests Mounting

30 Dead, 10 Missing, 65 Hurt In Train Crash In Montana; Bridge Sags In Cloudburst

U.S. Jury Indicts 18 As Spies In Reich Government's Pay; Secret Service Head Named

Lehman To Run For Senate; La Guardia Group Protests; Bennett In Governor Race

Louis Defeats Schmeling By A Knockout In The First; 80,000 See Title Battle

Lehman Calls For Purge Of Relief Rolls In State; Favors Curb On Spending

Roosevelt Plans Active Primary Role, Speaking Out For 'Liberal' Candidates; Rebukes Hague, Labor And Business

Italy Sends War Warning As Loyalists Talk Of Raids On Bombers' 'Home Bases'

100% Stalin Vote Ends Soviet Poll

Dewey Victory On Seizure Seen In Albany Debate

Dunnigan's Search Plan Loses, Dewey's Favored; Smith Aids Republicans

New Deal 'Purge' Said to Seek Control of House Rules Group

JULY

Roosevelt Warns Nations All Must Help Keep Peace; Extols Our Civic Liberties

Two Confess Murdering Snyder For Racketeers; $25,000 'Fixing' Reported

Fugitive General Agitates In Japan For Stalin's Fall

President At Gettysburg Sees Victory Near In Battle 'Fundamental As Lincoln's'

France Occupies Isles Off Hainan; Tokyo Perturbed

320 Die As Floods Sweep Kobe, Japan

War A Year Old, Gen. Chiang Urges Japanese To Rise

Arabs Clash With British On Trans-Jordan Border; Palestine Violence Grows

Roosevelt Aids Campaigns Of Barkley And Bulkley; Explains New York Deficit

Roosevelt Calls On Voters In Oklahoma And Arkansas To Elect Liberals To Office

Dewey Convictions Excel All Records Of Predecessors

President Hails 5 Texans, Makes Governor A Judge, Keeps Silent On Connally

Roosevelt In Colorado Gets Workers' Plea He Run Again; Ignores State's Primaries

Hughes Flies Over Canada After Brief Fairbanks Stop; Due Back Today, Inside 4 Days

Hughes Ends World Flight, Setting 3-Day, 19-Hour Mark; 20,000 Cheer Arrival Here

Hughes Acclaimed Wildly By Crowds; Gets City Honors

Pope Pius Assails Super-Nationalism As Breach Of Faith

Efficiency of the Nazis Stretches A 'Moving Day' to Two Months

Corrigan Flies To Dublin; U.S. Officials May Wink At Forbidden Hop In 'Crate'

Hitler Asks British Amity As King, Cheered In Paris, Stresses Ties With France

'Pickaback' Plane Spans Atlantic After Take-Off From Bigger Craft

U.S. Demands Arbitration Of Mexican Land Seizures; 'Neighbor' Policy At Stake

Britain And France Reject Hitler Sudeten Deal Offer Because It Omitted Czechs

Torrential Rains In The East Cause Heavy Damage; 8 Dead; New York Suburbs Flooded

Plane Rips Crowd, Kills 34, Hurts 150 At Columbia Fete

Gov. Earle Exhorts Legislature To Bar 'Judicial Invasion'

Youth 11 Hours On Ledge Leaps 17 Floors To Death As Thousands Watch Him

Britain Threatens Action To Protect Interests In China

TVA Head Upholds $680,000 Land Deal As Part Of Program

Pope Warns Italy Not To Hit Church In Race Campaign

Davis Will Plead Guilty And Testify Against Hines; Paroled In Care Of Dewey

AUGUST

Japan Claims New Rout Of Russians On Frontier; 250 Casualties In 2 Fights

103 Indicted Here In An Alcohol Ring; 6 Policemen Held

Soviet Hurls Six Divisions And 30 Tanks Into Battle With Japanese On Border

Japan Fears Raid, Cities Darkened; Fighting Renewed

Japan, Soviet Talk Peace But Moscow Insists Foes Must Accept It's 'Border'

Corrigan Captivates City; 1,000,000 Roar An Ovation In His Parade Up Broadway

Soviet Planes Raid Korea, Bombing Railway To Sea; Japan Threatens Revenge

Bolt Kills 3 At Riis Park, Injures 15, Repeating Tragedy Of A Year Ago

Fighting Is Heavy At Changkufeng; Japan Claims Hill

Soviet Artillery Blasts Enemy On 4-Mile Front; Japanese Await For Big Drive

Russia And Japan In Truce, Hold Lines Now Occupied; Agree To Delimit Border

Plane Here From Berlin In 25 Hours Without Stop After A Secret Take-Off

Organizing South's Wealth Vital To Sound Prosperity, Report To Roosevelt Says

Roosevelt Puts O'Connor And Tydings On Purge List; Left Wing Pressure Seen

Fascist Influence Growing In Mexico; U.S. Trade Suffers

Security Acts's Expansion Promised By Roosevelt; 'No Short Cut To Utopia'

Roosevelt Urges Defeat Of O'Connor And Tydings; O'Connor Accepts Fight

Hines Pointed Out In Court As 'Fixer' In Policy Racket; Gang Aid For Dodge Charged

Defiant Witness Is Jailed As He Charges Dewey Aides Forced Him To Accuse Hines

Policy Chiefs Say They Gave $15,000 To Tammany Drive, Put Hines Club On Payroll

Pope And Fascists Reach New Accord On Catholic Action

Tydings, Fighting Purge, Assails Federal Activity; Tells Of Vote 'Terrorism'

Witness Places Hines Aides At Policy Racket Quarters; Dewey And Pecora In Clash

Roosevelt Says G.O.P. Voting In The Democratic Primary Violates
Political Morals

Dodge Saw Hines Get $3,000 From Gang, Weinberg Says; Leader
Says Witness Lies

Riding Master Says He Saw Hines With Schultz In 1935;
Weinberg's Story Attacked

Weinberg, Ending Story, Denies He Slew Schultz; Brothwell Is
Unshaken

Hitler Warned By Britons That An Attack On Czechs May Result
in World War

British Cabinet Is Called In Growing Czech Strain; Envoy To Berlin
Returns

Britain Preparing To Warn Germany Anew To Shun War

Curry Swears Hines Asked And Got Police Transfers, Also
Nomination Of Dodge

SEPTEMBER

Davis On Stand Says Dodge Blocked Inquiry On Racket; Tells Of Gang Aid At Polls

Hitler Bars A Czech Truce; Henlein Takes Plane Home With New Counter-Demands

Berlin Sees No Early Crisis; Hears British Are Assured No Sudden Action Is Planned

Sudetens May Ask Berlin To Send Aid In Autonomy Fight

Cardinal Hayes Dies at 70 In Sleep at Country Home

Czechs Draft A 'Last' Offer; Concede Much To Germans; Henlein Stands By Demands

Reich Can Defy Blockade, Hitler Tells Nazi Rally; Silent On Czechoslovakia

Henleinists Break Off Negotiations Over 'Attack' On A Sudeten Deputy; Reich Attitude Reported Stiffening

Sudeten Outbreaks Add To Tension; Benes To Make Radio Talk To Czechs; British Still Debating Their Stand

Germany Will 'Capitulate To No One' Hitler Tells His Nazis At Nuremberg; Formal British Warning Reported

Goering Pledges Germans To Protect The Sudetens; Hitler Gets British Views

Nazis Insist On Annexation; Sudetens Want Plebiscite; Hiter To Tell Aims Today

Hines Mistrial Is Ordered After Month's Testimony; Dewey Rebuked By Pecora

Czechs Ignore Henleinist Ultimatum To Lift Martial Law In Sudeten Zone; Britain, France Press For Plebiscite

Chamberlain Off By Plane To See Hitler; Will Make A Personal Plea To Avert War; Prague Firm As Sudetens Battle The Police

Chamberlain Has 3-Hour Talk With Hitler; Paris Sees General Peace Conference Likely; Czechs Order Henlein Arrested As A Traitor

Czechs Will Fight To Hold Territory, Britain Is Told As Premier Returns; Hitler Awaits Pressure On Prague

British Cabinet Is Divided; Daladier Going To London; Czechs Decree Martial Law

Britain And France Accept Hitler Demands On Czechs; Will Ask Benes Today To Surrender German Areas; Prague, Incredulous, Regards Action As A Betrayal

Czechs Delay Decision On Partition; Ask French Attitude If They Refuse; Britain Seeks A Gesture From Hitler

Britain, France Give Prague Hours To Submit On The Peril Of Immediate German Attack; Czechs Are Declared Determined To Resist

Czechoslovakia Decides To Give Up; Crowds Protest, Cabinet In
Peril; Chamberlain To Demand Guarantees

Storm Toll 462; Thousands Homeless; 250 Killed In The
Providence Area; New England Still Battles Floods

Chamberlain Sends Hitler Terms To Czechs; Prague Completes
Mobilization In 6 Hours; Paris Cabinet Orders Partial Mobilization

Czechs Have Until Oct. 1 To Accept; Hitler Aids Polish-Magyar
Demands; Daladier Flying To London Again

Roosevelt Appeals To Hitler And Benes To Negotiate; British And
French Premiers Also Plan Plea To Reich; Terms Unacceptable;
Hitler Talk To Attack Czechs

Britain Pledges Aid If Czechs Are Attacked; Also Guarantees
Surrender Of Sudeten Area As Hitler In Speech Keeps Peace Door
Open

Roosevelt Appeals Again To Hitler As Hope Wanes; Reich Sets
Attack For Saturday, Denies New Deadline; Britain Mobilizes
Navy; Chamberlain Makes Final Plea

Hitler Warns War Moves, Calls 4-Power Conference; Meets
Mussolini, Chamberlain And Daladier Today; Munich Talk May
Cover Whole European Situation

Four Powers Reach A Peaceable Agreement; Germans To Enter
Sudeten Area Tomorrow And Will Complete Occupation In Ten
Days

OCTOBER

Britain And Germany Make Anti-War Pact; Hitler Gets Less Than His Sudeten Demands; Polish Ultimatum Threatens Action Today

Czechs Yield Area To Poles; British Naval Chief Quits; Europe Studies Alliances

Hitler To Accompany Army Into Sudeten Area Today; Britain Reassures France

Chamberlain Defends Pact Lends 10,000,000 To Czechs; Plans Talk With Mussolini

Geoghan Bank Accounts And Records Of 44 Aides Subpoenaed By Herlands

Benes Resigns Presidency On New German Pressure; Turn Toward Fascism Seen

Chamberlain Policy Upheld, No Conscription, No Election; Slovaks Obtain Autonomy

U.S. Asks Italy To Respect Rights Of American Jews; Retaliation Here Hinted

Vienna Nazi Mob Storms Cardinal Innitzer's Home; He Is Reported Injured

Hitler Announces He Is Demobilizing Army Reservists

Soviet Fliers Denounce Lindbergh As 'Hired Liar' for German Nazis

Japanese Launch South China Drive In Hong Kong Area

Japanese Ships and Planes Blast Way for Invasion of South China

Geoghan To Be Superseded In Brooklyn Graft Cases; Lehman Plans Full Inquiry

Lehman Promises To Serve Full Four Years In Office; He And Poletti Spurn Reds

Reich Impressed By U.S. Arms Plan; Baruch Denounced

Jerusalem Center Of Arab Attacks

Six Priests Seized By Nazis In Vienna; Prelate Is Curbed

7,200 Police Records Stolen At Brooklyn Headquarters; Sought For Graft Inquiry

Search For Thief Narrows In Brooklyn Police Scandal; Amen Gets 'Free Hand' Today

Brooklyn Inquiry Widened; Lehman Orders Amen To Act In Looting Of Police Files

Police Lieutenant In Jail As A Looter Of Records; 'Traitor,' Valentine Says

U.S. Navy Ignores Warning By Japan Of Peril Of Bombs

Aerial Bombs Hit A British Warship In Japanese Raid

Lehman Charges Falsity And Vilification To Rival; Dewey Assails O'Connells

Roosevelt Assails Dies Committee For Airing Charges Against Murphy; Chides Press On Wage-Hour Reports

Roosevelt Warns Nation Must Arm In World Of Force

U.S. Note Demands Japan Respect Rights In China; Insists On The Open Door

Germany Deports Jews To Poland; Seizes Thousands

Germany Ceases Deporting Jews Pending Parleys

Radio Listeners in Panic, Taking War Drama As Fact

NOVEMBER

18,000 At Labor Rally Here Hail Lehman And New Deal; Dewey Widens Racket Drive

Dewey, In Pledge To Labor Says Democrats Betray It; Lehman Sees Issues Evaded

La Guardia Will Support Governor; Lehman Calls Rival Civil Service Foe; Dewey Pledges Utility Rate Action

Dewey Declares Governor Fought Drive For Clean Government Here; Lehman Calls Crime Issue Hypocrisy

Roosevelt Appeals For Gov. Lehman, Wagner, Mead, Murphy Of Michigan; Links G.O.P., Fascists And Reds As Foes

Dewey Replies To Roosevelt Appeal; Charges Schultz Was Flynn Deputy; Lehman Says Foes Raise Race Issue

Race For Governorship Held Close; Wagner, Mead Lead On Election Eve; Mayor Denounces Religious Issue

5,000,000 Ready To Vote In State Today; Both Sides Confident In Close Finish; New Deal Facing Test In The Nation

Gov. Lehman And His Slate Elected; Big Republican Gains In The Nation; Earle, Cross Lose; Murphy Trails

Coalition In Congress To Halt The New Deal Urged As The Republicans Appraise Victory; Gain 80 In House, 8 In Senate, 11 Governors

Nazis Smash, Loot And Burn Jewish Shops And Temples Until Goebbels Calls Halt

Nazis Warn Foreign Press 'Lies' Will Hurt Reich Jews; Arrests Run To Thousands

Reich Bars Jews In Trade; Fines Them Billion Marks; Cardinal's Palace Stoned

Extremists Sway Nazis And Jews Are Menaced With More Drastic Rule

Washington Calls Envoy From Berlin; Chamberlain Plans To Ask Roosevelt To Join In Movement To Rescue Jews

Roosevelt Condemns Nazi Outbreak; 'Could Scarcely Believe' It, He Says; London Studies Jewish Colonization

British Ministers Approve Opening Colonies To Jews; Financial Aid Sought Here

Nazis Are Defiant As Rath Is Buried; Hitler Is Silent

Germany Recalls Its Envoy To Explain 'Singular' Stand Of Roosevlet On Nazi Acts

President Asks For Prayers For 'Unfortunates' Abroad; La Guardia Scores Dictators

Reich Police Raid Foreigners' Homes In Hunt For Jews

Britain Offers Reich Jews Land In Africa And Guiana;
$100,000,000 Fund Is Sought

Paris Receives Hitler Bid For 'Good-Neighbor' Ties; Chamberlain
There Today

Kennedy Helped Censor Newsreel, Commons Learns

British And French Agree On Strong Home Defenses; Will Build
Great Air Fleet

Pope Suddenly Stricken, But Condition Improves; His Doctors Are
Hopeful

Daladier Decrees Rail Mobilization To Combat Strike

Japanese Building Bases At Shanghai

President Returns Phillips To Italy; Silent On Germany

French Troops On Guard As General Strike Begins; Blum
Summons Deputies

DECEMBER

Daladier Defeats Strikers; Will Press His 3-Year Plan Of 'Economic Mobilization'

Daladier Decides To Call Parliament Into Session; Many Strikers Dismissed

France Protests Strongly To Italy On Land Demands

Germany Creating Ghettos For Jews Under New Decree

Latin Americans Demand Pact To Ban Use Of Force After Property Seized

Reich And France To Sign Anti-War Treaty Today; Paris Firm Toward Rome

France And Germany Adopt A 'Good Neighbor' Policy; Sign New Non-War Treaty

Mussolini Calls On Hitler For Assurance Of Backing In His Claims On France

France Increases Guard As Riots Spread In Tunis; Libyan Arabs Back Italy

Eden Calls On Democracy To Face World Challenge; 4,000 Give Him Ovation Here

Memel Vote Today Is Hailed By Nazis As Move To Reich

World Climate Growing Warmer, Say Russians, Citing Actic Data

Burns, Comedian, Pleads Guilty To Charges of Jewel Smuggling

Envoy And 35 Nazi Boycott Chamberlain At A Speech Rebuking The Berlin Press

Britain Warns Italian Pact Bars Any Attack On Tunisia; France Not To Yield 'An Inch'

4th U.S. Note Demands Reich Exclude American Citizens From Anti-Jewish Decrees

Coster Ends Life By Bullet; 3 Chief Aides Are Unmasked As His Brothers And Jailed

U.S. Obtains 'Proof' Of Big Arms Trade By Coster Concern

Many in Reich Deplore Excesses, But Fear Keeps Them Muzzled

Coster Contract To Sell 2,000,000 Rifles Revealed; Dewey Indicts 3 Musicas

Deranged Man Fells La Guardia, Who Fights Back, at City Hall

Coster's Note Put Blame On Himself; Brothers 'Stooges'

U.S. Rejects Reich Protest Over Ickes In Blunt Terms; Says He Uttered Our Views

Reich Press Turns Fire On Roosevelt For Jewish Award

21 American Republics Sign Pact To Resist Aggression; Warning To The Dictators

New Deal 'Waste' Denied by Eccles As He Assails Byrd

Paris Note Warns Rome Not To Invite Anyone To Mediate

Three Are Seized In Blackmail Plot Aimed At Coster

France Doubling Forces To Protect Somaliland; 2 Warships Are On Way

Chamberlain To See Pope On Plan For World Bloc To Oppose 'Pagan Force'

Reich To Build Submarines Up To Parity With Britain; Jolt To Chamberlain Seen

1939: NEW YORK TIMES (365)

JANUARY

Anglo-Reich Talks On Navies Halted Without An Accord

Peru Tried to Color News And Spied on U.S. at Lima

U.S. Agents Gather In Lima To Combat Fascists' Inroads

WPA Funds Were Used For Politics In 3 States, Senate Committee Finds; Congress Opens In Independent Mood

Roosevelt Offers A Defense Program Against Rising Menace Of Dictators; Threat Of Economic Sanctions Seen

Roosevelt Offers $9,000,000,000 Budget, With New Record Totals For Defense; Also Asks $875,000,000 For Relief Now

Senators Move To Control Relief Spending; Cut Of $200,000,000 Is Sought

Roosevelt Asks Democrats To Unite Behind New Deal; Urges Others To Join G.O.P.

Hungarians Renew Fight With Czechs In Frontier Areas

Move To Cut Relief Fund Makes Gain In Congress; La Guardia Asks For More

President Assigns Hopkins To Reconcile Labor Groups, Study Wagner Act Changes

Open Showdown On Relief Now Planned In The House;
$875,000,000 Bill Introduced

Vermont Votes Support To Gov. Aiken In Battle On Federal Land
Seizure

House In Rebellion Passes Relief Bill At $725,000,000; Restricts
Use Of The Funds

Revision Of Relief System Planned By Senate Group; Would Shut
Out Politics

Japan Now Facing U.S.-British Front On 'New Order' Idea

Roosevelt Asks Extension Of The Social Security Act To More Aged
And Children

Mexico Dispatches Envoy To Germany On Secret Mission

3,000 New Army Airplanes Authorized In House Bill; First Defense
Plan Step

Protecting Coasts From Air Invasion Is Key To Defense

Hitler Removes Schacht As Reichsbank President; Suspends
Refugee Talks

10 Of 13 Saved On Bermuda Plane Forced Into Sea On Hop From
Here; Picked Up By Tanker After 10 Hours

Rescue Ship Due Here Today With 10 Saved From Plane; Search
Ends For 3 Missing

Barcelona Placed Under Army Rule As Rebels Close In

Rebels Drive To Barcelona, Seize Airport, Shell City; Refugees Flee Northward

Quake Ruins 20 Chile Towns; Concepcion City Wiped Out; Loss Of Life In Thousands

Rebels In Barcelona Without A Fight; Hailed In Streets; Distribute Food; French Warn Italy On Her Demands

Roosevelt Lets France Buy Planes; Senate Inquiry On Policies Is Likely; Nazis Hint At New Demands By Hitler

Chamberlain Says Force Will Unite Democracies; Senators Hear Gen. Craig

Weinberg Suicide; Accuser Of Hines Used Guard's Gun

Hitler Demands Colonies, 'Riches' For Japan And Italy; Tells U.S. Not To Meddle

FEBRUARY

Roosevelt To Help Democracies Arm; Puts Our Defense Frontier In France; Tells Senators Of Dangers Abroad

Secrecy In Defense Policy Causes Stir In The Senate; Germans Attack Roosevelt

12 Dictators to Rule Britain in War, Each in a Self-Contained Region

Roosevelt Calls France Frontier Story A Lie; Denies Change In Policy; Attacks The Press; Secret Parley To Be Aired In Senate Debate

Peace Move By Loyalists Is Reported At Border; London As The Mediator

France Opens Her Border To Fleeing Loyalist Army; Azana Is On Way To Paris

Loyalists Modify Terms In Peace Talks At Border; Franco Bars Concessions

Loyalists To Continue War, Despite Loss Of Catalonia; French Warn On Intrigues

Madrid Makes Peace Move; France And Britain Prepare To Recognize Franco Regime

Pope Pius Is Dead At The Age Of 81; Cardinals At Bedside In The Vatican As End Comes In Sudden Sinking Spell

Body Of Pope Lies In State; World Leaders Pay Homage; Cardinals Prepare To Sail

Germany To Permit Jews To Re-Enter Trade Fields Until They Can Emigrate

Wallace Ridicules Reich 'Aryanism' In Talk On Lincoln

Hoover Warns New Deal Invites Inflation Danger; Party Rallies For 1940

Democrats Ask Roosevelt To Solidify Party For 1940 By Working With Congress

Rudich Dismissal Is Asked By The Amen Grand Jury; Calls Magistrate Unfit

German Envoy Urges Cardinals To Elect Pope Favoring Fascists

Roosevelt Tells Business No New Taxes Are Planned; Says Confidence Is In Order

Madrid Regime Asks Peace On Sole Basis Of Clemency; Defense Rushed By France

Minister Is Killed In Peru As His Coup Is Foiled By Troops

22,000 Nazis Hold Rally In Garden; Police Check Foes

Vinson Says Our Interests Link US To Britain, France; Commons Votes Arms Plan

Hitler Conveys to Chamberlain Pained Surprise at British Arming

Halifax Warns Axis Powers The Democracies Will Resist

Hopkins Declares Recovery Now Sought By Government With 'All Vigor And Power'

Hines Found Guilty On All 14 Counts In Schultz Policy Racket Conspiracy; Jury Out 7 Hours; Bail Is Continued

Mayor Act To Put Capshow Off Bench For Link To Hines; Sees 'Usefulness Impaired'

Supreme Court Outlaws Sit-Down Strikes, Upsets Labor Board Rulings In Three Cases; Hopkins Considers Wagner Act Amendments

MARCH

Mexicans Seize 8 In Nazi Spy Plot; Hunt Secret Radio

Franco Has Asked Italy To Recall Army In Spain, Bonnet Reveals In Paris

Pacelli Elected Pope On 63d Birthday; Named On 4th Ballot; Reigns As Pius XII; Expected To Continue Strong Policies

Pius XII Appeals For Peace In First Public Act As Pope; Sets Coronation March 12

Roosevelt Scores Return Of Religious Persecutions; Hughes Extols U.S. System

Gen. Casado Ousts Negrin; Heads New Madrid Council; Cartagena Revolt Quelled

Madrid's Council Headed By Miaja; Combats The Reds

A.F.L. Rejects Plan By Lewis For New Labor Federation; Leaders Meet Roosevelt

Britain To Put 300,000 Men In France In Event Of War; U.S. To Study Neutrality Act

Agreements With Brazil Lift Trade Restrictions And Renew Debt Service

STEPHEN BOEK

Germany Prepares To Act On Slovak Appeal For Aid As Prague
Ousts Premier

Maija Fights Reds And Nationalists; Revolt Persists

Pius XII Crowned On Balcony Before Vast Roman Throng; 4-Hour
Service Impressive

Hitler Reported Ordering Czechs To Set Up Three Independent
States; Sends Troops Toward The Border

Troops Of Four Nations Contend For Ruthenia As Hitler
Dissolves Czecho Slovak Republic And Makes Bohemia-Moravia A
Protectorate

Hitler Follows His Troops Into Prague; Czechs Jeer The Nazis; New
Regime Set Up; Hungarians Resisted In Carpatho-Ukraine

Slovakia Now Hitler 'Protectorate'; London And Paris May Recall
Envoys; Hungary Annexes Carpatho-Ukraine

Hitler Demands Trade Control Of Rumania; Chamberlain Bitter,
Drops Appeasement; Welles Condemns 'Wanton Lawlessness'

U.S. Raises Duties 25% On German Imports; Britain And France
Protest Czech Seizure; Russian Backing Sought In Bloc To Aid
Rumania

Rumania Accepts Hitler Trade Pact; Britain Is Sounding World
Power; Soviet Note Denounces Czech Seizure

Britain Seeks Anti-Hitler Compact; Russia Proposes Nine-Power
Parley; U.S. Won't Recognize Czech Seizure

Lithuania Yields Memel To Hitler; Britain Presses For 4-Power
Action; Fascist Council Backs Reich Policy

Hitler Sails For Triumph In Memel As Lithuania Signs Surrender
Treaty; Poles Block London Four-Power Pact

Hungarians Invade Slovakia; Hint His Program Is Ended Is Cut
From Hitler's Speech

Slovakia Calls On Hitler For Help Against Hungary; Poles Bar
4-Power Accord

Hitler Assures Mussolini Of Reich's Strong Support; Duce Defines
Policy Today

Mussolini Invites France To Discuss Colonial Issues; Paris Disposed
To Meet Him

French Bar Talk With Italy Pending Specific Demands; Germany
Pressing Poland

Madrid Yields, Ending War; Victors Enter Unresisted; Republican
Leaders Flee

Daladier Calls On Italy To Clarify Her Demands; Urges Anti-
Aggressor Bloc

Britain And France Decide To Defend Poland With Armed Power
If Germany Attacks Her; Act On Massing Of Reich Troops On
Border

APRIL

Chamberlain Pledge Heartens Poles To Warn Reich; Rumania Gets Offer; Berlin Shocked, Hitler Replies Today

Hitler Dares Britain To Pick Fight; Chamberlain Asks Duce To Mediate; London Gives New Assurance To Poles

Armed Pledge To Rumania Expected Today By London; Beck Arriving For Parleys

Britain Offers To Assist Any Land Menaced By Reich; Would End State Of 'Alarm'

Poles Agree To A British Alliance; Albania Threatened; Riots In Danzig; London Is Tense In Midst Of Rumors

Rome Hears Move On Albania Is Near; Italian And German Army Chiefs Meet; Axis Plans Warning To Democracies

Italian Forces Landing In Albania; Rome Reports Its Nationals Imperiled; Britain Offers Guarantee To Hungary

Albanians Resist The Invading Italians; Four Ports Seized; King Zog Offers Terms; British Protest; Berlin Backing Mussolini

Italians Take Tirana, King Zog Flees; White House Sees New Sharp Issue; British Studying Pledge To Greece

Britain Cautions Italians Not To Go Beyond Albania; Pope Hits Pact Violations

British Mediterranean Fleet Sails On Decision To Guard Greece, Turkey; Balkan Entente To Defend Frontiers

Britain Extends Defense Alliances; Poles Call Troops; Sofia Bans Nazis; Roosevelt Sees America Involved

Turkey Is Expected To Join The Anglo-French Alliance; Greece Is Holding Aloof

Britain And France Extend Guarantee To Rumania And Greece, Turkey Next; 'We'll Go Straight Ahead,' Says Duce

Roosevelt Calls For Peace In Europe, Says We Will Defend All Americas; Britain Presses For Russian Accord

Roosevelt Asks Dictators For 10-Year Peace; Orders The U.S. Fleet To Return To Pacific; Berlin Sees Rejection; Incredible, Says Rome

Nazis Fearful Of Effect Of Roosevelt Plea In Reich; Skillful Reply Is Expected

Reichstag Will Hear Hitler Answer Roosevelt April 28; British Confident Of Turkey

Britain Would Help Dutch, Swiss And Danes If Attacked; Reich Fleet Sails For Spain

Roosevelt Says Liberals Are Sole Hope For Party; Tells Others To Get Out

Mussolini Derides Roosevelt Appeal; Hitler Parades Reich Might At Fete; Soviet Proposal To Britain Reported

Secret Turko-British Pact Indicated In Fleet Moves; Russia Seeks
Triple Accord

Rumania In Reply To Reich Admits Lack Of Security; Other
Nations Deny Fear

Britain Unexpectedly Sends Envoy Back To Berlin Post;
Conscription Move Gaining

British Cabinet Agrees Unanimously On Conscription And May
Tax Wealth; Truce Offer By Hitler Seen Possible

Britain Gets Huge Defense Budget; Conscription Will Call Up
Millions; Hitler Snubs London's Ambassador

Nazis Make 3 Demands On Lithuania To Increase Turnover Of
Trade 25%; British To Conscript 200,000 Yearly

Roosevelt Asked Dictators To Confer With Him At Sea; Commons
Backs The Draft

Hitler Says No To Roosevelt, Insists On Danzig; Scraps Polish,
British Naval And Munich Pacts; Warsaw Defiant; Italy May End
London Treaty

1,000,000 To See Fair Opening; President To Speak At 2 P.M.;
Fleet Here, Visitors Pour In

MAY

President Opens Fair As A Symbol Of Peace; Vast Spectacle Of Color And World Progress Thrills Enthusiastic Crowds On The First Day

Hitler Assails U.S. Boycott; Appeals For Internal Unity; Poles Weigh Danzig Claim

Senators Fight To Hold Congress During Crisis Lest The U.S. Be Involved

Litvinoff Quits Soviet Post; Molotoff Foreign Minister; Britain For Pledge To Reich

Russia Switches Her Policy; Drops Collective Security; Foreign Capitals Puzzled

Beck Rejects All Of Hitler's Demands But Would Negotiate On An Equality; Britain Opposes Soviet Alliance Plan

Peace Move By Pius XII Reported As His Nuncios Consult High Officials

Reich And Italy Announce Plan For A Military Pact; Danzig Nazis Weigh Putsch

Pope Pius Asks Five Nations To Confer In Vatican City; Reich, Britain Woo Russia

Powers Cool To Pope's Plea; Danzig Showdown Expected; Britain To Be An Armed Camp

Russia Is Assured She Need Not Fight Until Britain Does

Chamberlain Warns Nazis Force In Danzig Means War; Soviet Still Wants Pact

British And Turks Proclaim Pledges To Aid Each Other

Program For U.S. In War Provides For 500,000 Men In The Aircraft Industry

Mussolini Declares War Unnecessary; Present Problems Do Not 'Justify' It; Roosevelt Studies Economic Parley

Senate Will Act On Taxes, Harrison Tells Roosevelt; White House Parley Lively

Roosevelt Urges Inquiry On Why Money Stays Idle; Says Recovery Is Retarded

King And Queen Welcomed In Colorful Quebec Rites; Empire Unity Is Stressed

One Dead, 180 Hurt In Palestine Riots Over British Plan

Franco Reviews 150,000 Troops; Rain Mars 5-Hour Madrid Parade

$150,000,000 Housing Voted As Legislature Adjourns; Budget Reduced $25,000,000

Pole Kills German In Danzig Disorder; Both Sides Protest

Axis Powers Sign Ten-Year Alliance To Remake Europe

59 Await Rescue On Sunken Submarine 240 Feet Down Near
Portsmouth, N.H.; Contact Restored After 10-Hour Break

33 Rescued From Squalus By Diving Bell; 26 Others Feared Dead
In Flooded Chambers; Survivor Tells Of Cool, Cheerful Discipline

No Hope For 26 In Squalus; Opening Of Hatch Reveals Water Fills
Their Section

Divers Clear Way To Raise Squalus; Pontoons Tested

Hull For Repeal Of Arms Embargo; Drafts U.S. Policy

Reich Church Head Defied By Pastors

75,000 March Today To Honor War Dead; G.A.R. Rank Thinned

Nazis Seize Palace Of Reich's Primate

JUNE

Russians Balk On Pact; Ask Anglo-French Pledge For All Baltic Neighbors

Manton On Stand Denies All Charges, Admits Gain Of $1,250,000 In A Year

Loss Of 86 In Submarine Feared As Tide Engulfs It; 4 Escape, Some Die In Effort

Judge Manton Is Convicted By Jury Of Selling Justice; Judge Martin Is Acquitted

Hitler Defiant Of Britain On 'Encirclement Policy'; Likens Her Aims To 1914

Hague Ban On C.I.O. Voided By The Supreme Court, 5-2, On Free Assemblage Right

Hitler Hails Deeds Of His Men In Spain As Lesson To Foes

King Enters United States; Hull Greets Him At Niagara; Due In Washington At 11 A.M.

King And Queen Guests At The White House After An Impressive Welcome In Washington; George Hopes We Will Ever Walk In Friendship

City Ready To Greet King And Queen Today; They Pay Homage At Tomb Of Washington, Visit Congress, Leave The Capital At Night

3,500,000 Cheering New Yorkers Greet King And Queen; They Are Officially Welcomed At Battery And Fair, Visit Columbia, Drive To Hyde Park For Day's Rest

King Departs For Canada; Attends Roosevelt Church And Eats Hot Dogs At Picnic

Drought Hits Near-By Areas Hard; Spring Rain the Least Since 1903

House Gets Neutrality Bill Favored By Administration; Arms Embargo Is Dropped

British Consider Reprisals For Blockade At Tientsin; All Concessions At Stake

Tokyo To Force Showdown On Concessions In China; Backs Army Over Tientsin

Britain Plans 'Active Steps' If Tension In Orient Grows; Warships To Run Blockade

British Hold Of Japanese In Clash At Shanghai Post; Tientsin Sees Long Siege

British Heartened On The Tientsin Issue; See Tokyo Pausing

Japanese Put Charged Wire Around British At Tientsin; Hull Defines Our Concern

Hull Protests To Japan On Kulangsu And Bombing; Action An Aid To Britain

Japan Orders U.S. Warship And Others Out Of Swatow; Yarnell Reported Refusing

U.S. Ships Ignore Japanese Demand; Hull Backs Stand

U.S. Gets British Rubber In Trade For Our Cotton; Seeks Deal With Belgium

Chamberlain Warns Reich Of British Military Might; Bars Japanese 'Dictation'

Nazi Acts Viewed As Prelude To War

Britain Advances Navy Manoeuvres To 'Danger Period'

Roosevelt Denounces Ban On Money Devaluing Power; Says It Aids Wall Street

Nazis Pouring Into Danzig From Reich To Join 'Army'; Young Poles Also Active

Britain Is Ready For War, Halifax Warns Germany; Poles Would Resist Coup

JULY

Hitler Plans Danzig Visit As Step Toward Regaining The City In 'Peaceful' Coup

British Labor Bids Germans Resist Nazi Warlike Aims; France Cautions The Reich

Chamberlain Again Warns Reich Against Aggression, But Is Silent On Danzig

Reich Denies Aim To Force Danzig Issue With Poland; Chamberlain Cites 'Influx'

Armed Forces Put At 10,000 In Danzig; Free City Is Calm

Roosevelt Dollar Control Restored By Senate, 43-39; He Maps Strategy For 1940

Frauds In City Sales Tax Bared With 5 Arrests; Chief Investigator Held

Senate Group Acts To Block Repeal Of Arms Embargo

90% WPA Shut-Down Here Threatened By A.F.L. Unions; Labor Unites For New Law

Nazi Leader Hurls Defiance In Danzig

Bills To Restore WPA Pay Are Offered In Congress; Thousands Back At Work

Senate Committee Votes For Delay On Neutrality; Roosevelt Will Fight On

Oustings By Italy An Anti-Spy Move; Anxiety Mounting

Trieste Leased By Reich For 10 Years, Swiss Hear; Troops Now Using Port

Roosevelt Asks Congress To Change Neutrality Act; Opponents Await Reaction

WPA To Drop 75,000 Here, Hire 42,000 On Home Relief; Move To Revise Law Ended

Japan Threatens Raid Into Siberia

Tyrolese Fight Evictions; 26 Are Reported Killed In Clashes With Fascisti

No Neutrality Revision This Session; Roosevelt Told By Leaders Of Senate In A Night Conference His Plea Fails

Names Of WPA Strikers Asked In Congress Inquiry; Links To Reds Are Sought

Inquiry Into Labor Board Voted By House, 254 To 134; Hatch Bill Is Then Passed

Revised Hatch Bill Passes Senate, Goes To Roosevelt; He Hits Neutrality Stand

War Games By Axis In Tyrol Forseen

Reich Now Admits Materials 'Famine'

Britain Concedes To Japan Rights To Security In China; Denies Belligerent Status

Japan Blocks British Trade By Closing River To Canton; Hull Won't Yield On China

U.S. Denounces Japanese Trade Treaty; Action Effective 6 Months From Now; Opens Way To Embargo On War Goods

Treaty Action Stuns Japan; Reprisals Hinted In Tokyo; U.S. Secrecy Irks London

Senate Economy Bloc Cuts Lending Bill By $850,000,000; Rejects Prevailing Wage

House Group Joins In Slash Of $850,000,000 On Spending; Dismissals By WPA Halted

Anti-British Drive Extended In China; Many Must Flee

AUGUST

3-Power Military Talks To Begin Now In Moscow; Spur To Political Accord

Lending Bill Is Killed In House, 193-166; Roosevelt Sees Recovery Retarded; Adjournment By Saturday Is Sought

$800,000,000 Housing Bill Faces Defeat As House Leaders Force Vote Today; President Warns On, Signs Hatch Act

Housing Bill Killed, 191-170, By House Economy Group; Quick Adjournment Sought

Congress To Adjourn Today; Deficiency Bill Increased By The Senate To $185,000,000

Congress Quits Sine Die At 6:35 P.M.; $119,000,000 More Voted For Crop Loans; Social Security Tax Cut $905,000,000

Japanese Destroy Two British Ships In Raid On Yangtze

Italy's War Games End Abruptly With Mussolini Strangely Absent

Angry Reich Press Threatens Poland With Mailed Fist

Yugoslavia Bars Axis Plan To Use Her Material In War; Danzig 'Plebiscite' Tonight

Fate Of Hungary An Issue As Ciano Goes To Germany; 'Protection' Assured Danzig

Ciano And Ribbentrop Meet; Confer With Hitler Today; Yugoslavia Calls Troops

Hitler, Ciano To Continue Conference A Third Day; Call Problems Complex

22 Killed, 60 Hurt In Crash Of Speed Train In Nevada; 'Sabotage,' Coroner Finds

Axis Reported Asking Pope To Call Four-Power Parley; Other Negotiators Active

Axis Warns Danzig Issue Must Be Faced Promptly; British Bar New 'Munich'

Germany Reveals Demands On Poland; Now Wants Both Corridor And Danzig; Press Asks Area Lost At Versailles

Reich Sees Polish Rebuff In Ignoring Of Its Terms; 'Action' A Matter Of Days

Reich Takes Over Slovakia; Puts Military In Control; Hungary Faces Nazi Crisis

Reich Calls Slovak Troops To Army On Polish Border; British Ministers To Meet

Poles Rush Troops To Face Germans; Pope Sends Peace Envoy To Warsaw; Berlin And Moscow Sign Trade Pact

Germany And Russia Agree On Non-Aggression; Ribbentrop Going To Moscow To Draft Pact; Berlin Sees Quick Showdown With Poland

Britain And France Stand By Pledge To Poles; Rush Plans For War; Warsaw Remains Firm; Elated Germans See Victory In Russian Pact

Germany And Russia Sign 10-Year Non-Aggression Pact; Bind Each Other Not To Aid Opponents In War Acts; Hitler Rebuffs London; Britain And France Mobilize

Hitler Acts To Take Danzig, Orders Army To Be Ready; Chamberlain Gets War Power; London, Paris Dark; Roosevelt Appeals To Germany, Poland And Italy

Hitler Reported Willing To Ease Demands On Poland; London Gets Terms Today; Britain And France Firm; Roosevelt Addresses New Peace Appeal To Germany

Hitler Demands Britain Abandon Polish Alliance; London And Paris Reported Rejecting Nazi Terms; Mobilizations Still Rushed; Nuremberg Canceled

Hitler Tells Paris He Must Get Danzig And Corridor; Berlin Thinks Door Is Left Open To Peaceful Solution; British Answer Today To Insist On Rights Of Poland

Hitler Gets British Note And Will Make Written Reply; Berlin Finds London's Stand 'Not Wholly Negative'; Tension Is Eased But Europe Remains Poised For War

New Hitler Note Keeps Negotiation Open; Berlin Hopeful For Peace, Slows War Moves; Commons Cheers Pledge To Resist Force

British Reply To Hitler Narrows The Issue To Free Negotiations With Poland Or War; Reich Organizes National Defense Council

SEPTEMBER

German Army Attacks Poland; Cities Bombed, Port Blockaded; Danzig Is Accepted Into Reich

Britain And France Send Ultimatums; Warsaw Calls Allies; Italy Neutral; Germans Attack Poles On 4 Fronts

Britain And France In War At 6 A.M.; Hitler Won't Halt Attack On Poles; Chamberlain Calls Empire To Fight

British Liner Athenia Torpedoed, Sunk; 1,400 Passengers Aboard, 292 Americans' All Except A Few Are Reported Saved

French And British Attack Germans On Wide Fronts; 2 Reich Battleships Hit In Air Raid On Wilhelmshaven; Stories Of Athenia Rescues Told; U.S. Curbs Travel

Germans Shell Warsaw, Residents In Flight; U.S. Neutrality Proclaimed, Arms Embargoed; Markets Here Rise; Athenia Was Shelled

Poles Hold Germans In Battle For Warsaw; French Invade Reich; British Land In France; Roosevelt Plans Early Congress Session

Germans Rush Troops West To Meet French; Polish Army, Intact, Still Defends Warsaw; Submarines Sink Four British Freighters

Germans In Part Of Warsaw, Poles Are Resisting; French Drive On, Report Saarbrucken Surrounded; U.S. Proclaims Emergency To Protect Neutrality

Germans Try To Sweep Around Warsaw Defenders; French Advance Again; Goering Makes Bid To Paris; British Cabinet Preparing For A Three-Year War

Poles Repel Attacks On Warsaw; Nazis Report Trapping 2 Armies; French Shift Their Drive In West

Poles Halt Enemy On Wide Front; French Continue To Gain In West; Reich To Intensify Shipping War

Nazis Say Warsaw Is Encircled; Poles Assert Foe Is Hurled Back; French Drive On Saarbruecken

Germans Bombing Open Towns, Britain Threatens To Retaliate; Nazi Offensive Gains In Poland

Russia Threatens Poland As Her Defense Crumbles; French Capture Prisoners

Russia And Japan Agree On Armistice In The Orient; Large Scale Battle Developing On Western Front; Drive In The East Is Slowed; British Sink Submarines

Soviet Troops Marched Into Poland At 11 P.M.; Nazis Demand Warsaw Give Up Or Be Shelled; Fierce Battle Is Raging On Western Front

Russians Drive 40 Miles Into Poland, Defense Weak; Polish President In Rumania, Warsaw Holding Out; Britain And France, Concerned, Consult On Action

Soviet And Reich Forces Meet, Map Polish Partition; 500 Lost On British Airplane Carrier Sunk By U-Boat; French Advance Within Outworks Of The Westwall

Hitler Tells Allies It Is His Peace Or A Finish Fight; Britain And France For War Till Hitlerism Is Ended; Russian Navy Reported Blockading Estonian Coast

Nazis Concentrate Forces In West; Brauchitsch Arrives From Poland; Britain Reports Czechs In Revolt

Roosevelt Asks Congress To Repeal Arms Embargo; Hard Fight Indicated As 24 Senators Map Resistance; Rumanian Premier Assassinated; Nazi Coup Foiled

Dutch And Belgians Open Dikes Seeing Threat In German Moves; Poland Partitioned By Invaders

French Repel 3 Counter-Attacks; Advance A Mile In Sierck Sector; Mussolini Would Halt War Now

Nazi Guns And Planes Razing Warsaw; Half Of City Is In Flames, 1,000 Slain; British Expect New Reich Peace Drive

French Shell Reich Forts On Rhine As Nazi Troops Mass Near Basle; Soviet Army At Estonian Frontier

Russo-German Pact To Dominate Balkans Seen In Moscow Parley; France Puts Ban On Communism

Estonia Reported Ready To Yield As Russo-German Parleys Begin; Warsaw, A Shambles, Surrenders

Reich And Soviet Join For Peace--Or War; No Buffer State; New Pact Warns Allies; Estonia Gives Moscow Sea And Air Bases

Britain And France Spurn Nazi-Soviet Peace; Formal Offer By
Mussolini Is Now Expected; Reich Hints Red Planes Will Attack In
West

OCTOBER

Reich Threatens To Sink British Ships On Sight; Holds Defensive Guns Make Them Warships; Ciano Is Invited To Berlin; Reichstag Called

Churchill Bars A Hitler Peace; Britain Conscripts 250,000 More; Latvia To Get Russian Demands

Senate Opens Battle Over Embargo With 60 Believed Favoring Repeal; Germany Warns American Shipping

Chamberlain Bars Hitler Pledges; Says Threats Will Not Sway Allies; Nazis See In Talk Chance For Truce

Turkey Resisting Russian Pressure For Dominant Role In The Balkans; Hitler Reichstag Speech Tomorrow

U.S. Refugee Ship Will Be Sunk, Reich Says, Implying Allied Plot; Hitler's Peace Terms Forecast

Hitler Demands His Peace Or A War Of Destruction; Allies Forecast Rejection, But Are Studying Terms; Russia Aloof, Reported Planning To Fortify Border

Roosevelt Cool To Mediator Role; Might Act Later If Sure Of Success; Britain Expected To Outline Terms

Soviet Agrees To Rush Goods To Reich As German Delegates Meet Molotoff; Paris Sees Hitler's Peace Misfiring

Finland And Russia Massing Troops; Sweden Sees Threat, Mans Defenses; British Navy Fights Off Air Bombers

Daladier Bars Peace On Nazi Terms; Finland Mobilizes Her Baltic Fleet, Sends Civilians From Border Towns

U.S. Reported Joining 3 Powers In A Plea To Russia On Finland; Anglo-Soviet Trade Pact Signed

War In Earnest Unless U.S. Acts, Berlin Says, After Chamberlain Rejects Hitler Terms; U.S. Appeals To Russia; Finns Plan For Worst

U.S. Ignores Nazi Mediation Plea; Berlin Asks Soviet-Italian Talks; British Sink Three More U-Boats

U-Boat Sinks British Battleship; 396 Of 1,200 On Royal Oak Rescued; Soviet-Finnish Accord Held Near

Submarines Sink Three Allied Ships; Shelled Without Warning; 15 Lives Lost; Turkey Rebuffs Moscow Balkan Moves

Nazis Bomb Navy Base In Scotland, Hit Cruiser, Kill 15, Lose 4 Planes; Germans Gain In Moselle Thrust

Nazis Attack With 100,000 On West Front; Planes Raid British Fleet And East Coast; Turks Reject Soviet Terms, End Parleys

Roosevelt Bars War Submarines From Using U.S. Ports And Waters; Scandinavia Weighs Aid To Finns

Turkey Signs 15-Year Treaty With Allies; Berlin, Moscow And Rome Are Perturbed; Scandinavians Urge Finns To Compromise

Berlin Says War Is On To The Finish; Hitler Calls Three Envoys To Confer; Allies Plan For Expected Nazi Drive

Nazi Planes Attack Convoy, 4 Downed; Hitler Orders A New Drive On Ships; Calls Party Men; Russia Warns Turks

French Quit Warndt Forest; Hold Only A Few Outposts; British Rout Air Raiders

Nazis Seize U.S. Ship City Of Flint, Sailing Her To Murmansk, Russia; Soviet Interns German Captors

U.S. To Demand Soviet Release Ship; Finns Halt Moscow Negotiations; Ribbentrop Assails Britain As Foe

American Crew Safe On City Of Flint; Russia Frees Germans, Holds the Ship; Nazi Press Urges Bombing Of Britain

City Of Flint, Freed, Quits Murmansk; German Crew Reported In Command; Passenger On Her Tells Of Capture

Pope Condemns Dictators, Treaty Violators, Racism; Urges Restoring Of Poland

Soviet Insists Flint Sailed; Berlin Reports Conflicting; Czechs Riot, Many Are Held

Flint's Route Held A Military Secret By Nazi Officials

Nazi Tortures Detailed by Britain; Concentration Camp Horrors Told

NOVEMBER

Molotoff Lays War To Allies, Berates US; Talk Angers Finns; U-Boat Attack Reported Off U.S.

White House Accuses Molotoff Of Meddling In U.S. Embargo Fight; No Trace Found Of Attacked Ship

House Dooms Arms Embargo, 243-181; $1,000,000,000 In War Orders Expected; Berlin Sees U.S. Taking Side Of Allies

Norway Interns German Crew, Frees Flint; Russo-Finnish Crisis Near; Embargo Repealed; Grew Threatens Economic Pressure On Japan

Roosevelt Establishes Combat Area; U.S. Nationals And Ships Barred In It; Reich Protest To Norway On Flint

Northeaster Pounds Coast Here; Rain Replenishes City Reservoirs

Reds Urge World Revolt, Include Reich As Capitalist; French Claim Air Victory

Democratic Sweep In City Election; Pari-Mutuel Amendment Is Adopted; California, Ohio Pension Plans Lose

Hitler Escapes Bomb Explosion By 15 Minutes; Six Killed, 60 Wounded In Munich Beer Cellar; $200,000 Reward Offered For The 'Instigators'

Fatal Border Clash Stirs Dutch; Defense Measures Are Rushed; Major Nazi Offensive Forecast

Lowlands Tense, Foreigners To Leave; Hitler Paper Expects Decisive Blow; Finland And Russia Are Deadlocked

Pius XII Criticizes Lack Of Religion In Schools Of U.S.

Britain And France State War Aims; George Says Aggression Must Stop; Lebrun Insists Nazis Return Spoils

Reich To Reply 'No' To Peace Proposal; Assures Neutrals

500 Reported Lost As Oil Fire Sweeps Town In Venezuela

Policeman Kills Long Beach Mayor, Shoots Bodyguard

General Motors Is Found Guilty In Monopoly Case

9 Czech Students Executed; U-Boats Seen Aiding Russia Set Up Blockade Of Finns

Mine Sinks Dutch Liner In North Sea; 140 Lives Feared Lost, 260 Rescued; Nazis Impose Martial Law In Prague

Mines Sink Five More Ships, Four Owned By Neutrals; British Plan To Sweep Sea

6 More Ships Sunk; British Weigh Ban On Reich Exports

Britain To Seize Reich Exports; Cruiser Reported Hit By U-Boat; Two Britons Held In Munich Plot

Mine Sinks British Warship, 40 Lost; French Craft Destroys Two U-Boats; Netherlands Halts All Ship Sailings

Report Nazis Drop Mines From Air; 9 Ships Sink; Allies Down 13
Planes; Rumania Names Pro-French Premier

Mines Forced London Port To Close, Holding Ships Outside Till
Cleared; Italy Joins Protests On Blockade

Nazis Bomb British North Sea Fleet; Report 4 Ships Hit, London
Denies It; Japan Threatens Blockade Reprisal

Soviet Charges Attack By Finns, Who Defy Demand To Quit
Border; Pilsudski And Armed Liner Sunk

Finns Offer Parley On Withdrawal; Soviet Urges Revolution In
Helsinki; Rawalpindi Sunk By The Deutschland

Russia Scraps Pact With Finland; Three Border Clashes Reported;
British Raid German Naval Base

Russians Start Their Invasion Of Finland; Planes Drop Bombs On
Airfield At Helsinki; War Starts As U.S. Move For Peace Is Made

DECEMBER

Finns' Cabinet Resigns As Soviet Bombs Cities; New Government Expected To Seek A Truce; Russia Seizes Port And Islands; 200 Are Killed

Soviet Sets Up Red Regime On Finnish Border; Finns Rally, Report Sinking An Enemy Cruiser; Roosevelt Condemns 'Wanton' Russian Attack

Finns Report Soviet Drive Halted; Red 'State' Meets Moscow Terms; Roosevelt Bars Planes To Russia

Finns Ask For Peace Negotiations; Say Mines Killed 1,000 Russians; British Airplanes Raid Helgoland

Russia Refuses Peace, Spurns League; Finns Check Invasion, Fortify Alands; British Ship Victims Of German Raider

Finns On Offensive, Raid Enemy Bases; Swedes Call Troops, Mine Sea Coast; U.S. Would Join In Denouncing Russia

Red Organ Calls On Rumania For Pact Similar To Those With Baltic States; Moscow Reports Break In Finns' Line

Russians Blockade Finland; Balked At Mannerheim Line; Italy Warns On The Balkans

Kennedy Presents To President Plan To Use Idle Ships

Finns Hurl Back Russians In Attacks On Wide Front; Four More
Ships Are Sunk

U.S. Gives Finland $10,000,000 Credits; Helsinki Appeals To
World For Help; Disputes Soviet Claims Of Advances

League Calls On Russians To End War And Negotiate; Finns Hold
Back Invaders

Russia Rejects League Demands, Presses Drive In Central Finland;
Bremen Eludes Foe, Dashes Home

British Defeat Nazi Raider In All-Day Fight; She Runs To
Monevideo With 36 Dead, 60 Hurt; U-Boat Sunk, Reich Cruiser
Hit In North Sea

Uruguay Lets The Spee Stay For Repairs As British Mass Warships
Off Montevideo; Finns Report Gains; League Drops Russia

Spee Must Go By 6:30 P.M. Tomorrow; Finns Report Suomussalmi
Retaken; British Planes Raid German Bases

Spee Still In Harbor At Daybreak Although Ready For Dash To Sea;
Reinforced Allied Fleet Awaits Her

Captain, On Hitler's Order, Sinks Spee Off Montevideo After
Debarking Crew; Finns Report 20,000 Russians Trapped

Air Fleets Fight Off Helgoland; German Cruiser Sunk In The Elbe,
British Submarine Hits 2 Others

Liner Columbus Scuttled Off U.S.; Nazi Freighter Flees To Florida;
Russians And Finns In Air Raids

Columbus Crew Held At Ellis Island; Captain Of Graf Spee Kills
Himself; Tanks And Airplanes Attack Finns

Russians Retreat In Arctic From Finns, Cold And Snow; Raid
Helsinki Hospital Zone

Finns Press Retreating Foe; Rome Hears Of Peace Talk; Nazi Fleet
Reported At Sea

Taylor Named Peace Ambassador By Roosevelt To Work With
Pope; Finns Victors On Central Front

Pope Offers 5 Bases Of 'Just Peace'; Urges 'Right To Life' Of All
Nations; Finns Drive Ahead On Three Fronts

Nation, At Peace, Unites In Thanks On Christmas Day

Finns Repel Foe In Karelia; Viborg Again Is Bombarded; Rumors
Stir Russian Public

Finns Again Cross Border, Imperil Russian Railroad; Soviet Calls
More Troops

Quake Casualties 110,000, Turk Investigators Say

3,000 Russians Die As Finns Beat Off Karelian Attacks

Finns Drive Russians Back Over Border For Third Time; Hitler
Asks For Sacrifices

ABOUT THE AUTHOR

Stephen Boek is the founder and curator of the Ministry of Truth Archive, a website dedicated to headlines from different news sources. Stephen has spent the last three years collecting headlines from over a hundred years ago and headlines from today. He is not paid by any media sources and collects his work independently. Stephen once walked around in Portland wearing a MAGA hat when he realized that sometimes the news is not exactly the way it is presented. If you have time to read other years or other news sources he shares them at ministryoftrutharchive.com